The Pink Toolbelt

The Pink Toolbelt

Spiritual Remodeling for Women

Mary Dodd

A DEVOTIONAL

carpenter's guide
PUBLISHING

ISBN 978-0-9980172-0-4

Cover Design by Jeanette Gillespie, Jam Graphic Design
Interior Design by Beth Shagene
Edited by David Lambert for Somersault
Author Photo by Korey Howell Photography

Manufactured in the United States of America

17 18 19 20 21 22 • 19 18 17 16 15 14 13 12 11 10 9 8 7 6 5 4 3 2 1

Contents

Acknowledgments   11

Introduction   13

PHASE ONE: The Right Tool for the Job

1. Spiritual Safety Goggles   17
2. Use Your Hammer for Construction, Not Destruction   21
3. Pull That Nail and Patch That Hole—Restitution   24
4. The Spiritual Tape Measure   27
5. Follow the Blueprints   31
6. The Spiritual Safety Harness   34
7. The Hard Hat of Salvation   37
8. Sturdy Work Boots   41
9. A Shield of Faith   44
10. A Toolbelt Full of Prayers   46
11. Praise and Worship   49

PHASE TWO: The Boss and the Foreman

12. Who Is God?   55
13. YAHWEH's Attributes   59
14. A Good Father   62
15. Who Is Jesus?   64
16. Messiah Fulfilled the Spring Feasts of YAHWEH   67
17. Messiah Will Fulfill the Fall Feasts of YAHWEH   70
18. All That Messiah Has Done   73
19. True Discipleship   76
20. Think Like Messiah   78

21. Be Like Messiah   81

22. Forgive Like Messiah   84

23. Serve Like Messiah   86

24. Resist Temptation Like Messiah   88

25. Trust in Jesus—the True Messiah   91

PHASE THREE: Apprentice under the Holy Spirit

26. The Holy Spirit   97

27. The Spirit of Wisdom and Counsel   100

28. The Spirit of Knowledge and Understanding   103

29. The Spirit of the Fear of YAHWEH   106

30. What Are My Spiritual Gifts?   108

31. God's Intricate Design for My Life   111

PHASE FOUR: Christlike Attitudes

32. Blessed Are the Poor in Spirit   115

33. Blessed Are Those Who Mourn   118

34. Blessed Are the Meek   120

35. Blessed Are Those Who Hunger after Righteousness   123

36. Blessed Are the Merciful   126

37. Blessed Are the Pure in Heart   128

38. Blessed Are the Peacemakers   130

39. Blessed Are Those Persecuted for Christ's Sake   132

PHASE FIVE: Be Transformed, Not Conformed

40. Evidence of the Remodel   137

41. Fulfilling the Father's Will   140

42. Meeting the Needs of Others   143

43. I Can't Do This by Myself   145

44. Don't Resist Advice   149

45. Show Gratitude for Timely Help   151

46. Contaminated Ground? Get Rid of It! 153

47. Be Honest 156

48. Be a Light 158

49. Daily Conversations 161

50. When You Don't Feel Like Loving 164

51. The Kingdom Perspective 166

52. Apply Kingdom Thinking to Your Faith 170

53. Apply Kingdom Thinking to Your Job 174

PHASE SIX: Build through Good and Bad Weather

54. Finding Courage in Christ's Example 179

55. Keep an Eye on Each Other—Intercessory Prayer 182

56. An Active Faith 184

57. Draw Near 186

58. Dress for the Weather 189

59. Be Diligent 192

60. I Don't Understand—Why Me? 194

61. Triumph through Tragedy 197

62. Dig Drainage Ditches 199

63. Clean Up the Site 202

PHASE SEVEN: Completion and Final Inspection

64. What Should My Finished Project Look Like? 207

65. Room-by-Room Inspection 209

66. Am I Done Yet? 212

67. Now I See Dimly 214

68. Crown of Life 216

69. Occupancy Certificate 218

70. Keeping Your Eyes on the Skies 221

Author Bio 225

Acknowledgments

Thank you to my parents. You have given me the greatest gift of all—you led me to Christ.

Thank you to my parents-in-law for giving me my second-greatest gift—my darling, Tony.

Sweet husband Tony ... thank you, thank you, thank you for sharing your life with me—what a ride!

Thank you Ginny, AJ, Cole, Emily Jo, and Michelle—you make this momma happy. I love you!

To the chubby brothers, and to Spark-plug and Boo—this MIMI loves the stuffing out of you!

Thank you to the Somersault team for your invaluable insights and expert guidance through this publishing experience, and thank you to my editors, David and Cindy—genius times two.

Introduction

I AM A CARPENTER. AS FAR BACK AS I CAN REMEMBER, I'VE BEEN fascinated with anything construction-y. In fact, fresh out of high school, I joined a traveling construction crew that disassembled, moved, and then reassembled the big blue silos seen all over America's heartland. It was hard work and great fun. Shortly after that, I got married. Before long my husband and I started our own construction business, and I joined him on many of our own construction sites. Together we have built everything from huge horse-riding arenas to massive log homes. I love building stuff—you might say I have sawdust running through my veins.

Because I also love to write, I thought it would be a great idea to combine my two loves and write a devotional book based on construction analogies. So I started this book with great energy and zeal. But after a few short months, the bottom fell out of my perfect little world when my family reached a breaking point.

My marriage had been a struggle for many years, and now one by one I had lost connection with most of my precious children. Our family barreled down the fast track toward hopelessness and destruction, and try as I might, I could not put on the brakes and stop what was happening. Chaos set up camp in my heart. I felt wooden and hopeless. Sorrow, anxiety, and self-blame became my new and constant companions. I did not like them much.

In that time of desperation, Father God offered me an epiphany—a gift of revelation that changed my spiritual course forever. It was a gift so simple even a child could understand it, and yet profound enough to change the world. It's a gift that continues to rock my socks off to this day.

Be a true disciple of Christ.
That's it.

The very day Father dropped this truth into my spirit, I decided to apply it to every single area of my life, no matter how small. That was the beginning of a radical change in me. Slowly, day by day, my life began to be transformed into the image of God's Son. And in the process my marriage, my parenting practices, and my important relationships were transformed as well.

My thoughts, my attitudes, my actions—and the biggie, my words—were challenged in my overall effort to become like Christ. I was determined to serve like Christ, to become the least and last, and to go the extra mile—even when it was difficult, even when it was inconvenient. My decision and the resulting effort, along with the enabling power of the Holy Spirit, had an effect: My spiritual eyes were opened. And following in the footsteps of my Savior, I started to see humanity—especially my husband and my children—through His eyes instead of mine.

The decision to be like Christ in *everything* has touched *every* area of my life. This carpenter who built and remodeled houses for a living began a period of *spiritual remodeling*. Nothing has been harder to implement, yet nothing in my life up to this point has been more rewarding.

Because of the change this decision brought to my life, I invite you —no, I *implore* you—to join me on the job site of *spiritual remodeling*. If you decide to strap on a toolbelt (yes, a *pink* one, ladies!) and learn to be like Christ in every minute area of *your* life, then you too will be amazed at how much authentic spiritual growth you'll experience. Your life will change as you begin to be transformed into the image of Christ. Your socks, like mine, will be completely rocked off this planet.

So strap on that pink toolbelt, find a new pair of socks, and let's get started!

MARY

The Right Tool
for the Job

Use a screwdriver to pound in a nail and you'll discover it doesn't work well for the job. The only reason you would even try it is if you didn't know where your hammer was. Not only is it important to have the right tool, but it is equally as important to know where all your tools are.

The same is true for spiritual remodeling. You need to know which spiritual tool is right for the job and how to put that tool to work—instantly.

Spiritual Safety Goggles

Shall we indeed accept good from God
and not accept adversity?
—JOB 2:10

LIKE JOB, I HAVE HAD MY SHARE OF TRIALS.

At twelve weeks into my fifth and final pregnancy, I had a miscarriage. Devastated, my husband and I went to my doctor for help. Our sadness was softened by the incredible news he gave me: "You're still pregnant." Unbeknownst to me, I had been carrying twins. I had lost one precious child that night, but because my "surprise" twins were in separate amniotic sacs, the other twin still rode safe and sound within. We cried over our loss and laughed over our surprise.

All was well until only halfway through the length of a normal pregnancy, I went into labor and began to hemorrhage. Terrified, we rushed to the emergency room. The doctors successfully stopped the contractions, but the hemorrhaging continued. I was admitted to the hospital for a nice long stay. The staff prepared us for the worst as we prayed and hoped for the best.

For four more weeks, delivery was averted, giving my baby a chance to grow and mature. Every day in the womb gave her a better chance of survival. But one night the hemorrhaging became so severe we all knew delivery was imminent. Three-and-a-half months premature, my little angel entered the world.

She weighed only one pound ten ounces—about the same weight as six sticks of butter. She was so tiny and fragile I was afraid to touch her, lest I cause her unnecessary pain.

The first month of her life was touch and go. One day, as I sat crying next to her isolette in the Neonatal ICU, I thought of Job. *Lord, I prayed, our lives are in Your hands. Please help my daughter live. But even if You choose to take her home, I will never stop praising You.*

That wasn't an easy prayer, because I desperately wanted to hold her and kiss her and keep her forever. But I knew God's plan was best, and that outside of His will I would be miserable. As hard as it was, I submitted my will to His and praised Him, even though I didn't know what the outcome would be. I let the pain of the trial make me stronger.

I look back on this as one of my greatest victories. My daughter is now twenty-one years old, as sassy as they come, and a musical genius to boot!

That experience has now become a habit: Whenever I'm hurting, I think about Job, a man who was blessed with much but whose whole world came crashing down around him in just one day. He was so miserable that even his wife encouraged him to curse God so he could die and be finished with the agony. Yet through all the heartache, pain, and temptation to quit, he stayed faithful to the Almighty. Even though he didn't understand why it was all happening, he concluded, "Shall we accept good from God, and not trouble?" (Job 2:10 NIV). Job lamented his circumstances, but he never stopped blessing God. He knew much more was going on than his spiritual eyes could see. You could say Job was wearing a pair of spiritual safety goggles.

When I'm at a construction job site, I wear safety goggles to protect my eyes from whatever dangerous object might become airborne. The goggles also allow me to keep my vision focused and clear. Just as *construction* safety goggles protect our *physical* focus, *spiritual* safety goggles protect our *spiritual* focus. They help us keep our eyes on God's bigger plans.

Life has a way of throwing obstacles at us. That's why our spiritual safety goggles are so important. They keep our eyes from lingering on our own problems, even though they're swirling all around us, and enable us to stay focused on God's eternal big picture instead. They help us say, "God, I don't understand this, but I trust that You are in control. I bless Your holy name!"

Christ always wore His spiritual goggles. We see evidence of them the night of His greatest trial, when His earthly world was caving in. His best friends betrayed Him, the spiritual leaders were hunting Him down so they could get rid of Him, and the Roman government granted their wishes even though they had found Him not guilty of the crimes for which He was accused. Christ's anguish was so terrible and deep that His sweat became like great drops of blood falling from His brow. Even so, He prayed, "My Father, if it is possible, let this cup pass from Me; yet not as I will, but as You will" (Matt. 26:39). He knew God saw the bigger picture. He knew God's will was best. And He continued to praise God despite great anguish.

What a perfect example Christ is to follow. Because He trusted His Father's will during His greatest trial, we too can trust our Father's will during our greatest trials. We can wear our spiritual goggles with great confidence—knowing God sees the bigger picture and all we need to do is trust Him and cling to Him.

Spiritual goggles helped me get through one of the most challenging times of my life, and I know they will help you get through your most challenging times as well. Follow our Savior's perfect example and keep those spiritual goggles glued to your face.

Final Thoughts and Questions

- What circumstances has life thrown at you that take your focus from Father's bigger picture?

- How will you keep your spiritual safety goggles glued to your face today?

Prayer

Father, I submit my will to Your will. I trust that You are in control of everything that concerns me. Help me to keep on my spiritual goggles so I can focus on You and Your will, even amid a storm-filled life. Amen.

Day Two

Use Your Hammer for Construction, Not Destruction

With the tongue we praise our Lord and Father, and with it we curse human beings, who have been made in God's likeness. Out of the same mouth come praise and cursing. My brothers and sisters, this should not be. Can both fresh water and salt water flow from the same spring?... Can a fig tree bear olives, or a grapevine bear figs? Neither can a salt spring produce fresh water.
—JAMES 3:9–12 NIV

OUT OF SHEER BOREDOM AND FOR ENTERTAINMENT'S SAKE, OUR crew and I have names for many of our tools. The tall wooden ladder is appropriately named Woody, the little blue pry bar is called Shorty, and the green circular saw is Mean-Green (he's kind of temperamental). I even have a name for my favorite hammer—Sally. Sally's grip fits my hand perfectly, she is light enough that my un-muscled biceps can wield her effectively, and her claws pull nails as if they were in butter. I love my hammer and get pretty upset if she's not where she's supposed to be—in my toolbelt.

The truth is, without my hammer I couldn't build. Hammers are essential to construction. They can be used positively to secure the fasteners, and they can also be used for demolition. The words we speak are the "hammers" we use in spiritual remodeling. These "hammers" should only be used to build the relationships in our lives—with God and man. Sometimes, though, we use them to demolish and destroy.

Too many times we use our words like destructive sledgehammers. In one breath we're praising God, but in the next we're cutting down our children or spouse—or anybody who frustrates us.

The careless use of angry words has been a struggle for me in the past. When I was frustrated, my words became hammers of destruction, injuring whoever was near, usually the people I love the most. How sad!

This problem plagued me for years, and I felt powerless to fix it. But one day, as I asked the Holy Spirit to help me tame my sinfully destructive tongue, Father God showed me a simple truth. I sensed Him saying, *The way you speak to Me is the same way you should speak to others. You cannot build your relationship with Me without building it in the same manner with others.* Immediately I remembered the parable in Matthew 25:40, where Christ says whatever we do to the least of these, we do to Him.

I was stunned—and deeply convicted. I repented and made a conscious decision to be aware of my every word: *What am I saying? Why am I saying it?* There is something eye-opening about consciously listening to myself speak. Sometimes it isn't a nice revelation, but I'm glad for it nevertheless, because through it I gained victory over my unruly tongue.

Loving God and loving others go hand in hand. Jesus said the two greatest commandments are "Love the Lord your God with all your heart and with all your soul and with all your mind and with all your strength" and "Love your neighbor as yourself" (Mark 12:30–31 NIV).

Jesus never used His words to destroy. He always used them in love to teach others, to instruct, and sometimes even to confront bad attitudes. But even when confronting someone, His motive was always complete love. And because of His words, the world is changed for the better. His words brought life and light to the earth. His words show us how to get to Father and how to please Him. Jesus used His spiritual hammer wisely—for construction, not destruction. Most importantly, He used His words to show God how much He loved Him.

As His disciples, we must follow His perfect example and be like Him in every area of life—especially with our words to God and our fellow man.

Final Thoughts and Questions

- Do I wisely use my words to bless and build? Do I ever use words like a destructive sledgehammer, hurting or manipulating those who are near? Why?

- When I fellowship with God, what words do I use? Do I use the same kind of words when I fellowship with others—my family and those close to me?

Prayer

Father, I want to show You today how much I love You by using my words to build up others, not destroy them. Help me to bless You and others with my words. Help me to be a good spiritual remodeler today. Amen.

Day Three

Pull That Nail
and Patch That Hole—
Restitution

*Zaccheus stopped and said to the Lord, "Behold, Lord,
half of my possessions I will give to the poor, and if I have
defrauded anyone of anything, I will give back four times
as much." And Jesus said to him, "Today salvation has come
to this house, because he, too, is a son of Abraham."*
—LUKE 19:8–9

BESIDES A POUNDING SIDE—THE SIDE YOU HIT A NAIL WITH—
hammers also have a "nail-pull" side. Our spiritual hammers have a
"nail-pull" side also, and when our words have been hurtful because
we've used them destructively rather than constructively, we need our
spiritual nail puller to pull the harmful words back out. We do this by
going to the person we've hurt and asking for forgiveness. This is never
easy, but it's a crucial process every relationship needs if it's to survive.

When a nail is mis-pounded and then pulled back out, it leaves a
hole. And on a piece of exterior trim, it is vital to patch that hole to
prevent moisture from getting in and causing dry rot. Spiritually, when
a word has been mis-pounded, the act of seeking forgiveness is like
pulling the harmful word back out. But even after the offending word
is "out," unless that hole is patched, sin and resentment can penetrate
the hole and cause relationship rot. We can patch the hole by making
restitution for the pain we've inflicted. It is never good enough to say,
"I'm sorry." We must also show our sincerity by making amends.

Restitution: *The act of restoring to the rightful owner something that has been taken away, or, the act of making good or compensation for loss, damage, or injury* (www.thefreedictionary.com)

Restitution is one of the pillars of our faith, spoken of throughout both the Old and New Testaments. But unfortunately, it is much forgotten and overlooked today. In fact, we are often taught that seeking forgiveness for our sins and getting baptized is all the Christian life requires. But according to Leviticus 6:5, "Anything about which he swore falsely; he shall make restitution for it in full and add to it one-fifth more. He shall give it to the one to whom it belongs on the day he presents his guilt offering." Restitution must take place if we want to have complete right standing before the Almighty!

In fact, our salvation story is based upon the restitution principle. We sinned and created a chasm between ourselves and a holy God. Jesus Christ came and made restitution for us—redeeming us and restoring us to Father.

Luke 19 tells a beautiful restitution story. Zaccheus, a crooked tax collector—meaning he stole freely from the people he collected from—was convicted by the Holy Spirit to restore funds to those he had defrauded. Zaccheus obeyed the Holy Spirit's prompting and decided to restore four times what he'd stolen, even though the Mosaic law required only that he restore the amount plus one-fifth its value. Zaccheus went above and beyond what was required. Christ's love, as well as the working of the Holy Spirit, reminded Zaccheus of God's principles. He listened and was changed! Christ rewarded his changed heart by saying, "Today salvation has come to this house" (Luke 19:9).

Christ taught us to seek forgiveness from the ones we have harmed. And He wants us, as disciples of Christ, to take it further by making restitution. And when we make restitution, we can remember the debt He resolved for us. We owe Christ everything for what He did for us on the cross.

Final Thoughts and Questions

- Do you have unresolved tension between you and someone because you've failed to pull out your destructive words?

- If so, how can you effectively make restitution?

Prayer

Father, bring to my mind people whom I have harmed with my words. Show me how to ask for forgiveness, but even more, show me how I can patch the hole I've caused. Help me make restitution and restore fellowship. Amen.

The Spiritual Tape Measure

What use is it, my brethren, if someone says he has faith but he has no works? Can that faith save him? If a brother or sister is without clothing and in need of daily food, and one of you says to them, "Go in peace, be warmed and filled," and yet you do not give them what is necessary for their body, what use is that? Even so faith, if it has no works, is dead, being by itself.
—JAMES 2:14–17

SOMETIMES MY MEASURING GETS ALL MESSED UP! AS A RESULT MY projects sometimes turn out a bit—shall we say—wacky.

Not long ago, as I was trying to trim out an interior door, I had to recut the top trim board three times because each time I cut it too short. No matter what I did, I just couldn't get it right. In the end, I succumbed to failure and put it up regardless of its imperfection, and I then used a tube of wood putty to fill in the gaps. It looked okay. Not great, but passable. However, the boss was not happy! I was not happy! The door was not happy!

You must admit, though, it's hard to read all those little lines. My eyeballs protesteth loudly. But I know my projects might have a better result if I slowed down and put my glasses on so I can read the tape measure accurately, instead of saying, "Three inches and five-ish of the littlest lines."

It's easy to fall into the same problem when we try to measure our faith. Faith, I believe, has become a confusing subject. Sometimes we think believing in something strongly enough is what faith is all about. Sometimes we think faith is the ability to control God, or even the adherence to a certain doctrine. When we don't spend enough time studying the subject—or we rely on unbiblical opinions about faith—our lives can get turned upside down. The result is a spiritual house that does not resemble what we want it to look like. And sometimes it can look like my trim board—a wee bit wacky. Our faith has failed because we did not measure it correctly.

But faith does not have to be tricky, wacky, or confusing. When we let Christ teach us about it, our measuring will be perfect and spot-on! Jesus shows us what true faith looks like, acts like, sounds like, and loves like. When we look to our Messiah and let *Him* show us what faith is, the Holy Spirit enlightens our thinking and clears up the confusion.

What did Christ say about faith? He praised the centurion in Matthew 8:8 who said, "Just say the word, and my servant will be healed." The centurion recognized that God worked through Christ in a mighty way, and he accepted it as truth. Christ commended his faith by saying, "Truly I say to you, I have not found such great faith with anyone in Israel" (v. 10). Likewise, Christ was overjoyed at the friends of the paralytic man who opened the roof and lowered their friend before Jesus, who immediately healed the man and forgave his sins. Their actions revealed to Jesus their genuine faith. Sincere faith creates sincere actions. Faith is active!

Christ had great faith in His Father. He said in Luke 18:27, "The things that are impossible with people are possible with God." He lived this statement out to its fullest when He healed the sick, raised the dead, multiplied fish and bread, stopped storms, walked on water, and defied matter. His faith was alive and full of works and actions. So too must our faith be. Our faith should look more and more like Christ's faith every day.

Our faith in the Father propels us into "works" that build God's kingdom here on earth. We work hard to push back the darkness. We work hard to show God how much we love Him. We know salvation comes only through following the Messiah, Jesus Christ, and we work hard to show Him our belief and trust in Him.

Correctly "measuring our faith" requires us to ask,

- Do I really know God, or am I floating along with a vague understanding of Him?
- Do I believe He created all things?
- Do I understand His ways?
- Does God feel known by me?
- Am I trying to ride on the coattails of my parents' or grandparents' faith?
- What are my beliefs?
- What do my actions say about my faith?

Final Thoughts and Questions

I invite you to make this your statement of faith:

I, _____, on this day, _____, do pledge my life in service to YAHWEH God, my King. I am His servant, and He is my Master. I put my complete trust in Him, knowing that He loves me and wants me to grow in spiritual wisdom and might. I pledge to study His divine Word so that I can understand His divine truths. I place my complete trust in the fact that Jesus the Messiah died for my sins. His blood covers my guilty death sentence. I am saved through Jesus's blood. I trust that Father God sees my attempts to live a righteous life and that He will reward me for my faith. I pledge to work hard to build God's kingdom, push back the darkness, and be a light for YAHWEH and His beautiful, holy Son!

Prayer

Father, I surrender my will to Your will. Help me to remember that You are in control. I will seek after You and strive to live a life that resembles Christ. I believe You see my faith in You and will reward it as You see fit. Help me to have an active faith that lives out my trust in You. Give me opportunities to pray for the sick, help the hurting, and clothe the poor—knowing that when I do, I am working out my faith in You. Amen.

Day Five

Follow the Blueprints

The word of God is alive and active.
Sharper than any double-edged sword,
it penetrates even to dividing soul and spirit, joints and marrow;
it judges the thoughts and attitudes of the heart.
—HEBREWS 4:12 NIV

I HAVE WATCHED MANY LOVED ONES FALL AWAY FROM THEIR FAITH. It's distressing to see and intensely painful in every sense. But in each case I have observed a systematic progression: first, the demotion of Christ's role as Messiah and Redeemer, and then a subtle devaluing of God's Word.

The spirit of humanism and atheism, which opposes God and all His ways, is stealing away our children one by one. Their generation worships science instead of the One who created science. They call good evil and evil good. They don't want to be tied down and constrained by truth, so they say truth is determined by how you feel. Because they have lost sight of the truth of God's Word, they have traded the truth for a lie.

This is nothing new. Mankind has been doing it since the beginning. But it is especially painful when our own children are caught up in that unholy flow. It breaks my heart!

Even so, there is good news. God's promises, as revealed in His Word, are true. He promised if we raise our children in the truth, in the end they will return. And don't forget Matthew 24:35: "Heaven and earth will pass away, but My words will not pass away." All untruth will fade away, and its lies will disappear. Hallelujah, truth wins!

Not only is God's Word ultimate truth, it is in fact like a blueprint for our lives. When I'm building a home, I rely heavily on the blueprints for every step I make in the process. I know every board and beam has a purpose and a place in that home—some for bearing large amounts of weight, some for stability, and some for practicality. The blueprints show me that every board and every nail work together to create something solid that will last a lifetime.

This blueprint—God's Word—has been and always will be the most powerful weapon we can use against the Enemy. The truths of the Word are the most powerful tools in our toolbelts. The Word has something to say about every area of life. It was breathed out and spoken into being by God, its author. The Bible is spiritually correct, and in its original state it is without error. Even if translation errors exist, God's perfect truth is always revealed when Scripture is compared with Scripture to reconcile itself.

God's Word is alive and active. Not only does it separate truth from lies, but it sends the Enemy packing. That's why it's so effective to pray the Word. Speak it over your children. Quote it out loud. Pray it over your spouse. Speak it over your circumstances.

Some of my own family no longer believe the Bible is the ultimate truth, so I pray the Word over them. I know, beyond any doubt, that it is going forth and accomplishing what it's supposed to do. It is convicting of sin, it is dividing truth from lies, it is drawing my family back, and it is defeating the Enemy.

Final Thoughts and Questions
Suggested prayers for your children and grandchildren:

- *I declare that my children are taught of YAHWEH.* (Isa. 54:13)

- *I declare that my children are growing in wisdom and have favor with YAHWEH and man.* (Luke 2:52)

- *I have trained my children in the way of YAHWEH, and His Word promises that when they are old they will not turn from it.* (Prov. 22:6)

- *Thank You that Your angels will keep charge and accompany my children and defend them and preserve them.* (Ps. 91:11)

- *I plead the blood of Jesus over my children and grandchildren.* (Rev. 12:11)

Suggested prayers for your spouse:

- *Give my husband wisdom and courage to find his source of life in You; help him to remember that You are always with him.* (Eph. 3:16)

- *Show my husband what it looks like to love me as Christ loves the church.* (Eph. 5:25)

- *Give my husband wisdom and revelation.* (Eph. 1:17)

- *Bring great fruit. Help my husband obey Your Word and depend on You.* (Gal. 5:16–22)

Prayer

Father, help me to love and obey Your Word. Help me to treasure it and use it daily as a weapon against the Enemy. Give me understanding as I read it. Amen.

Day Six

The Spiritual
Safety Harness

*Beware of the false prophets, who come to you in sheep's clothing,
but inwardly are ravenous wolves.*
—MATTHEW 7:15

If you love Me, you will keep My commandments.
—JOHN 14:15

I WORK ON SOME STEEP-PITCHED ROOFS, AND I'M PRETTY CLUMSY. Roofs are not good places for fumblers like me. Before I began building homes, I worked on a farm silo construction crew. Working on top of eighty-foot-tall silos was even scarier than working on home roofs (okay, a *lot* scarier). Being that high in the air is especially terrifying. Of course, if I'd had on a safety harness, I might have been a wee bit braver.

Wouldn't it be great if we had a *spiritual* safety harness—something that would keep us from falling, keep us attached to God, and help us to be confident in our walk before God? Something that would tell us how to live righteously? Such a thing exists: the teachings of Jesus.

Christ's teachings are a set of instructions for living. They were the spiritual safety harness for the early church, and they are our spiritual safety harness today as well. Anything other than Christ's teaching is false teaching. We must beware.

Jesus taught directly from His Father's Word, and at that time His Father's Word consisted of what we know today as the Old Testament.

It's interesting to note that He didn't do away with any of His Father's Words, but instead taught the people how to interpret them and apply them properly. In some cases, He even challenged the people to a higher level of observance.

Christ loved and was completely dedicated to His Father's Word. It was as if He brought fresh revelation directly from heaven as to how the Word should be lived out to produce the maximum amount of blessing in our lives. In a sense, He taught us not to ignore but to *magnify* his Father's instructions. He said in Matthew 5:21–22 (paraphrased), "You heard it said, do not murder, but I say do not even be angry." He also said in verses 27–28 (paraphrased), "You heard it said do not commit adultery, but I say do not even look at anyone with lust."

As disciples of Christ and as living temples of YAHWEH, let's hook up our spiritual safety harness so it can keep us from falling away from God. Let's learn everything Christ taught, apply the lessons, and keep them strapped on as we spiritually remodel our lives. Father is pleased when He sees that safety harness doing what it was created to do.

Final Thoughts and Questions

Christ completely obeyed and honored all of God's commands. The most famous commandments are the Ten Commandments: Worship only the Lord your God; do not make idols; do not use the name of God irreverently; observe the Sabbath and keep it holy; honor your father and mother; do not murder; do not commit adultery; do not steal; do not lie; do not be envious. As a spiritual remodeler, you must recognize that your safety harness is hooked up properly only when you are making every effort possible to live out the teachings and actions of Christ. The quickest way to lose the safety harness is to start to follow the teachings of men and women instead of the teachings of Christ.

Christ was hard on the spiritual leaders of His time—not because they were teaching God's Word, but because they would add to and subtract from God's Word. Christ got upset when they put their own spin on His Father's concepts. This sort of thing still goes on today. And that is why when we follow the teachings of mere human beings, our safety harness slips off and leaves us in spiritual danger.

> ## Prayer
> *Father, help me to honor Your instructions as taught by Your Son. Teach me Your ways, and teach me how to rise to a higher observance. Amen.*

Day Seven

The Hard Hat
of Salvation

*"What man among you, if he has a hundred sheep and
has lost one of them, does not leave the ninety-nine in the open
pasture and go after the one which is lost until he finds it?
When he has found it, he lays it on his shoulders, rejoicing. And
when he comes home, he calls together his friends and
his neighbors, saying to them, 'Rejoice with me, for I have found
my sheep which was lost!' I tell you that in the same way, there
will be more joy in heaven over one sinner who repents than over
ninety-nine righteous persons who need no repentance."*
—LUKE 15:4–7

I'M ONE OF THOSE PEOPLE WHO REGULARLY WHACK THEIR HEADS. I get into "ram mode" and start moving too quickly. My husband cringes when he sees me do that, because he knows sooner or later I'm going to run right into something, and it's going to hurt. And he's right—I do and it does. A lot! It's a real problem—one my head isn't happy about. But at least as far as damage to my head is concerned, that problem would go away if I would just strap on a hard hat.

Would you be surprised to learn that we have a *spiritual* hard hat? The helmet of salvation (Isa. 59:17) is a hard hat that not only saves our noggin but preserves our eternal souls. We should go through every single day with this spiritual helmet strapped on and secure—our eternal soul depends on it. Why? Because sin separates our souls from God, creating a deep spiritual chasm between Him and us. And because every human sins, none is exempt from God's judgment. We all deserve the death sentence. Instead of death, though, our merciful Father wants us to live—with Him—forever. He offers us a hard hat to protect us from the consequences of our own mistakes.

From the beginning of time, God made plans to extend His mercy to His children through the promised Messiah. And through this Messiah—Jesus—we can share a relationship with such a holy God. Only through faith in Jesus, through sincere repentance and complete discipleship (being like Christ) can we be confident of our salvation.

The stories of Jesus we're familiar with—His birth, His miracles, and so on—are all found in the New Testament. But the Old Testament is also all about Messiah. It is full of pictures and hints of Him. For instance, Moses the redeemer is a picture of Jesus the Great Redeemer. The Levitical role of the high priest, a mediator between Holy God and sinful man, is a foreshadowing of Christ's role in relation to the church. Also, Isaac's *willing* sacrifice on Mount Moriah (did you know he was thirty-seven years old and still a willing participant?) is a foreshadowing of the Messiah's *willing* sacrifice on a hill called Golgotha.

Not only does the New Testament teach us about salvation through a blood sacrifice, but the Old Testament does as well. Before God came to earth as a man, salvation was found through genuine repentance, a sincere effort to follow the ways of God, and through the blood sacrifice redemption as explained in the Mosaic law (Leviticus). Jewish men often were baptized in a Mikvah, an ancient pool of water, to show their desire to be clean of their sins. In Matthew 3, John the Baptist preaches the message of "repent and be baptized." The fruit of repentance was critical to John.

In verses 7–8 of Matthew 3, some religious leaders who often twisted the teachings of God came to John for baptism. He tells them, "You brood of vipers!... Produce fruit in keeping with repentance" (NIV). I believe the fruit of repentance John referred to is obedience to God's commandments (with nothing added to or taken from them)—with a contrite heart that understands its own need for redemption.

The New Covenant's way to salvation is not much different.

- **Believe in the blood sacrifice.** Matthew 26:28: "[Jesus said,] 'This is my blood of the covenant, which is poured out for many for the forgiveness of sins'" (NIV).

- **Baptism**. Acts 2:38: "Repent, and each of you be baptized in the name of Jesus Christ for the forgiveness of your sins; and you will receive the gift of the Holy Spirit."

- **Repentance.** Acts 3:19: "Repent and return, so that your sins may be wiped away."

What is required of us is a genuine belief that only the pure blood of Messiah—Jesus Christ—can cleanse us of our sins, followed by baptism, which reveals the 'fruit of repentance.' This is the start of the transformation process.

As you can see, it is not as simple as reciting the sinner's prayer. Although reciting the sinner's prayer is the appropriate way to start, it is meant to be the beginning of the process Paul describes as working out our salvation with "fear and trembling" (Phil. 2:12). Salvation is supposed to change us completely. Yes, it is a free gift, but we must follow Christ's instructions to redeem it. We have nothing in us that deserves this kind of gift—we deserve death. But because of God's grace and His great love for us, we can change our spiritual direction. We can have *transformed* lives.

Old Testament or New Testament, the Word is all about Jesus the Messiah. He is the way to the Father. He is our perfect example of living, praying, reacting, interacting, loving, and being. He is the narrow path to God. When we follow His fine example, we can confidently stay on that narrow path. This pleases the Father and causes Him to rejoice as He writes our name in His Book of Life.

Final Thoughts and Questions

- Is any sin standing between you and God?

- Do you believe in your heart that Jesus Christ is the Son of YAHWEH?

- Have you repented of your sins, accepted the blood sacrifice offered to you by Jesus, and made a commitment to follow Him for the rest of your days—demonstrated through the public proclamation of baptism as an adult?

Prayer

Father, thank You for giving me Your perfect Son. I love Him and will serve Him all the days of my life. Reveal to me the sins I need to repent of. Help me to live like Christ. Help me to strap on my spiritual hard hat of salvation every day. Amen.

Day Eight

Sturdy Work Boots

Put on the full armor of God, so that you will be able to stand
firm against the schemes of the devil.... Stand firm therefore,...
having shod your feet with the preparation of the gospel of peace.
—EPHESIANS 6:11, 14, 15

EARLY IN MY CAREER IN CONSTRUCTION—BELIEVE IT OR NOT—I
wore sneakers at work. One day a heavy sheet of metal came crashing
down on my sneaker-clad big toe. When I finished hopping on one
foot, yelling in pain, my poor toe still throbbed with every heartbeat.
Its painful pounding caused me to walk gingerly for several days and
sleep even worse, until finally the toenail turned purple and fell off.
Yuck! Since then, I have faithfully worn heavy-duty work boots every
single workday. I have thoroughly learned my work-boot lesson.

Spiritual work boots are just as important. In fact, the first thing
a general will examine is his soldiers' footwear. He wants them clad
in boots that are tough and sturdy, laced up and ready for marching.
The general knows the path on which his platoon will be marching
could be rough, uneven, and rocky. He wants his soldiers ready for
battle—not limping and distracted. He wants to win the war, and his
key to doing that is soldiers who are prepared.

Our Father too wants us laced up and ready. He wants us to win
the war we daily wage against evil. Because of Christ, we are now
enlisted in God's army, and we are being sent out to fight God's
battles. To do that, we need good, sturdy boots that won't give out
on us. Ones that won't leave us limping along. Ones that will help us
win the war.

In other words, we need our feet shod "with the preparation of the gospel of peace" (Eph. 6:15).

We fight the war by sharing Christ's redemption story. We fight the war by being like Jesus, which means acting like, thinking like, speaking like, showing kindness like, and loving like Christ. Isaiah 52:7 says, "How beautiful on the mountains are the feet of those who bring good news [or the gospel of peace]" (NIV). When you are being like the Son, your feet bring the gospel of peace.

When we're living and sharing the gospel of peace, we're women in harmony with the universe because we are at peace with God. And when we have made peace with God through Christ, we have the deepest sense of peace. Yes, we are still waging war, but we don't let the circumstances of war rattle us. We know to whom we belong. We know who wins! We keep marching onward.

Christ wore His spiritual work boots. He was at peace with His Father. He kept His eye on Father even during extreme hardship. His feet never slipped. He never gave up or quit marching. He never limped along. He was ready for whatever Father gave Him to do.

Final Thoughts and Questions

Dear sister, please don't stop marching. Don't stop fighting evil. Don't stop sharing the gospel that brings true peace. Lace up the proper spiritual work boots our General requires. And don't be afraid to wear them every day.

By the way, they look good with any outfit and fit like a glove. So much more comfortable than high heels. Just saying!

Prayer

Father, help me to cover my feet with Your Son's gospel of peace. Help me as I fight evil. Help me as I push back the darkness. Help me share Your Son's story with boldness and zeal, so that everyone who hears my words will be drawn to You. Amen.

Day Nine

A Shield of Faith

*In addition to all, taking up the shield of faith
with which you will be able to extinguish
all the flaming arrows of the evil one.*
—EPHESIANS 6:16

IN ANCIENT TIMES, A SHIELD WAS AN IMPORTANT DEFENSIVE TOOL.
It protected the wielder from flaming arrows and close-proximity
sword attacks. The shield Paul is speaking of in Ephesians 6:16 is
more like a door—long in shape and heavy, similar to a moving wall.
It was probably covered in metal sheeting so flaming arrows would
bounce off.

Fire falling from the sky is a dreadful thing for any soldier to
face. Likewise, we should not treat Satan's arrows lightly. They have
wounded many believers and taken out many other souls. When we
start relying on our own strength and think, *These arrows will never
take me down*, that's when we are in the greatest danger of that very
thing happening. The Enemy is always lurking, waiting to use whatever he can against us. That is why we must shield up daily—hourly
even—against his tactics.

What are some of Satan's "flaming arrows"? The list includes
temptations many of us find appealing: lust, greed, pride, self-focus,
anger, lying, adultery, and slander. Those are biggies for sure, but how
about overeating, little white lies, gossip, envy of bigger and better
material items, selfish manipulations, or bigotry?

All these arrows are serious. They should have us running to
God—and using our faith in Him as our shield.

Our faith in God enables us to look at temptation through a spiritual lens, meaning that we are able to see past the lure of the sin to its end result: *This temptation will cause me to sin against God and will result in putting distance between Him and me.* We can foresee the pain the sin will bring to God and to others. Our faith in God helps us to love Him enough to say, "I cannot *and will not* sin against God in this way."

We all have our individual weaknesses to temptation. One of the flaming arrows the Enemy often launches at me is financial anxiety. The faith shield I raise is this: I recall all the times God has taken care of me. For example, because of His provisions I have never missed a mortgage payment, and I have never missed a meal for lack of food. Nor have I ever had to beg for anything. My God has always taken good care of me, and I *know* He will continue to take good care of me forever. This shield of faith extinguishes Satan's financial-worry arrows every time!

Final Thoughts and Questions

- What arrow is the Enemy throwing at you right now? How has Father God proven Himself faithful in this area in the past?

- Let remembering His times of provision strengthen your shield of faith.

Prayer

Father, my faith in You is my shield. I hide behind Your protection and trust You with all my cares and burdens, knowing that You are supreme and all-powerful. I love You. Amen.

Day Ten

A Toolbelt Full of Prayers

*"Whatever you ask in My name, that will I do,
so that the Father may be glorified in the Son.
If you ask Me anything in My name, I will do it."*
—JOHN 14:13–14

OVER THE YEARS, MAKING PRAYER A PRIORITY IN MY LIFE HAS BEEN a great struggle. I wanted to have alone time with God, but it just wasn't happening. Granted, I was a mother to five busy children, so quiet time alone—with God or by myself—was almost nonexistent. But now that my children are grown and a little less needy, I have finally conquered this goal. And I'm so glad I did. Being alone with Father is not only precious to me, but it has become a lifeline to which I cling with white-knuckled fists and eyes clenched shut. Prayer is what keeps me together.

Trying to learn more about prayer, I found that I had to go way back in time to get the big picture. Here is what I found:

God's original plan for Adam and Eve was that they were to have dominion over all the earth (Gen. 1:26–28). But when they disobeyed, their sin had devastating consequences—death and destruction. When a covenant child of God prays in Jesus's name, the curse of death and destruction gets foiled because prayer releases the Holy Spirit to do God's will on earth. And His ways are for life, peace, and joy.

Before Christ came to earth, man was able to access God only through the help of a high priest. This high priest played an important role in the life of God's people. He was the mediator between a holy God and an unholy people. Hebrews 9:11 clearly tells us that Jesus put an end to the Levitical high priesthood because a superior High Priest has been installed—Jesus. Jesus shows us the way to the Father. He is our mediator. In some ways, nothing has changed—we still need a high priest to gain access to God. But in other ways, *everything* has changed—we now have a High Priest who is the perfect Son of God, one who has suffered and been tempted just as we suffer and are tempted. He is a high priest like no other. He is a high priest who is the Holy Son of God—the King of heaven. He is a high priest who is well acquainted with our earthly plight, and because of that He lovingly takes our prayers directly to Father. He is a high priest born of heaven. He is the High Priest.

We can look at prayer as a type of heavenly court session. The Great Righteous Judge—God Almighty—sits on the throne. Christ, our advocate, is the righteous lawyer who is constantly defending us before the Great Judge. And Satan, the great accuser, is daily accusing us before the Great Judge. But when we pray and ask forgiveness of our sins, Christ—our Great Defender—covers our sins in His precious blood. Therefore, the accuser can no longer make his case stick. All our sins are acknowledged and forgiven. This allows us to go boldly before the Great Judge and ask in Jesus's name for things such as healing, restoration, life, provisions, good gifts, the saving of souls, and ultimately His perfect will. Our prayers can now be heard and answered, thanks to the Great Defender—Jesus.

Prayer is a great privilege purchased by the blood of the Messiah. Looking at prayer from this perspective makes it a magnificent honor of epic proportions—one I am so grateful for!

Final Thoughts and Questions

Christ knew the importance of prayer. He taught us how to pray, and His model for prayer covered it all: praise and adoration for our

Creator and provider, allowing Father's will to be done in our lives, deliverance from evil and temptation, and the forgiving of sins, our own and others'. I encourage you to make the Lord's Prayer (Matt. 6:9–13) a part of every prayer session.

Prayer

Father, holy is Your name. May Your kingdom and Your will be done in my life. Thank you for all Your provisions—I praise you for them. Forgive my sins in the same measure that I forgive others. Lead me not into temptation and deliver me from evil.

You are my Righteous Judge. You hear my prayers. Thank You for my mediator—Jesus Christ—who always defends me before You and gives me the privilege of coming before You with my praises and my requests. I am so very grateful. I love You. Amen.

Day Eleven

Praise and Worship

About midnight Paul and Silas were praying and singing hymns
of praise to God, and the prisoners were listening to them;
and suddenly there came a great earthquake, so that the
foundations of the prison house were shaken; and immediately all
the doors were opened and everyone's chains were unfastened.
—ACTS 16:25–26

I HAD AN *AHA* MOMENT THE OTHER DAY. YOU KNOW—ONE OF THOSE moments when head knowledge suddenly becomes heart knowledge? In my aha moment, I realized that when I worship God, my worship of Him ministers to *His heart.* My worship blesses Him! Words cannot describe the impact this heavenly epiphany had on me. It made me stop and examine my own quiet times with God. Was I spending enough of it in worship of Him? It quickly became obvious to me that I wasn't, so I expanded the worship part of my quiet time. Now worship takes up half of it, and prayer takes up the rest.

I believe praise is a key that opens heaven to our prayers. Praise makes our prayers more powerful and sends the Enemy packing. Judges 20 tells the story of when eleven of the tribes of Israel went up against the tribe of Benjamin. The high priests inquired of God, and in verse 18 He told them to send Judah first. *Judah* means "praise." In other words, when ancient Israel went into battle, they would send the worshipers first. Praise is a weapon of spiritual warfare. It brings victory—spiritually and physically.

Praising Father for a favorable outcome *before* the battle even takes place is a definite act of faith: *I can't see the physical answer to prayer yet,*

49

but I praise You Father God for the favorable outcome nonetheless. After all, anyone can offer praise once the battle is won, but it takes a person of great faith to praise God before the outcome is evident.

When Joshua and the Israelites came to the city of Jericho, God directed Joshua to send seven priests blowing seven shofars to march around the city walls. Now, a shofar is significant for many reasons: it calls the people to attention, it is an instrument of spiritual warfare, and most significantly, some teachers believe that its sound is the sound our souls make to God—a sound without corruption, a sound of pure praise. These priests blowing shofars led the ark of the covenant and the whole procession of God's people, who praised and worshiped while they marched. We know how that story ends: the people shouted with a great shout of praise, and the shofars blew their praise to God with a mighty blast that made the walls of Jericho fall flat. This was Israel's first major victory in the Promised Land. What a great lesson they learned that day—praise causes all walls of adversity to come down. The same is true for us today,

Paul and Silas were beaten with rods, thrown into an inner prison, and their feet fastened in the stocks. Yet amid physical pain and misery, they sang hymns and praised Father. Suddenly there was an earthquake, and all the prisoners' chains came loose and doors were opened. Their decision to praise the Almighty, even during some really bad circumstances, must have been a major reason for God's intervening to create this miracle.

Final Thoughts and Questions

Singing songs of praise and worship to Father God is a powerful tool we all need to keep in our spiritual toolbelts. Is it in yours?

Prayer

Father, I extol Your beautiful name. You are holy, perfect, unchanging, merciful, and the essence of love and perfection. I love You with all my heart, soul, and might. May my worship of You bless Your beautifully holy heart. I want nothing more than to please You! Amen.

PHASE
TWO

The Boss
and the Foreman

We can't afford to ignore two important people on a construction site: the boss and the foreman. A worker performs better when she understands her boss's expectations. And when she understands her foreman's instructions on how to meet those expectations, productivity increases greatly.

The same is true on the spiritual construction site—we must know what Father God wants, and we must understand Jesus Christ's instructions as to how to accomplish it. When we do, the result is great spiritual growth and kingdom productivity.

Who Is God?

"God is spirit, and those who worship Him
must worship in spirit and truth."
—JOHN 4:24

I ONCE HAD A FRIEND WHO TOLD ME SHE LOVED JESUS BUT DIDN'T understand or know the God of the Old Testament. Her statement shook me to the core, because I realized that was true of me as well. It caused me to dig in to get to know the God of the Old Testament— our Father.

I suspect that, sadly, many believers can identify with my friend's statement. If you're one of them, I want to introduce you to the Great Creator of the universe. I want you to love Him, know Him, and understand His ways. I want you to worship Him in spirit and in truth, as Jesus explained in John 4:24.

How do we worship God in spirit and truth? I believe that *truth* part is learning who He is and what His real name is, and coming to understand His character. It is knowledge of the One we are worshiping. Without true knowledge of Him, our worship is dry, on the surface, and emotionless. The more we understand God, the more that truth enters our worship.

And here is some of that truth: God's ancient Hebrew name is YAHWEH (Ya-way). His holy, blessed, and revered name is set apart and above every other name. It is to be worshiped, but never to be spoken in vain. His name is to be acknowledged, written about, and heralded from the mountaintops and among the nations as the name of the One True God! (Ex. 9:16)

Consider these aspects of our God:

- **He is invisible** (1 Tim. 1:17). He is a spirit without shape or form, who operates outside time and space. In fact, all of creation resides within Him.

- **He is the Creator** (Gen. 1:1). He made the unique, beautiful woman you are. He loved you so much that He fashioned the sunrise, the stars, and all the earth just for you.

- **He is the Deliverer** (Ps. 18:2). Whatever circumstances you face, He can and will deliver you. In fact, He is so big that all problems are tiny to Him.

- **He is the Most High** (Gen. 14:18). No one is higher than God. He has all authority over you and your circumstances. That means you can trust Him with *everything*.

- **He is the Almighty** (Rev. 1:8). He has *all* the power.

- **He is the One True God** (Deut. 6:4). There is no one else. Only YAHWEH is God!

- **He is eternal** (Deut. 33:27). He is the same yesterday, today, and forever. He is unchanging.

- **He is the Rock and Fortress** (Ps. 18:2). You can count on him to *always* surround you and *never* leave.

- **He is merciful** (Lam. 3:22–23). His mercies are new every morning.

- **He is avenging** (Nah. 1:2). He is not happy that the Enemy is always trying to trip you up. He is your defender.

- **He is jealous** (Ex. 34:14). He longs to commune with you and is jealous when you forget about Him.

- **He answers prayers** (John 15:7). Always! The answers may not be exactly what you want, but He always hears and answers them.

- **He is the living God** (Jer. 10:10). He is alive, and all life comes through Him. Nothing can exist outside of Him.

- **He is perfect in all His ways** (Ps. 18:30). He is the ultimate perfectionist. He pays attention to the minutest of details, like freckles, eyelashes, and fruit flies.

- **He is righteous** (Ps. 145:17). There is no wrong in Him.

- **He is steadfast** (Lam. 3:22–23). He never stops.

- **He is the King and ruler of all** (Ex. 15:18). He is the king of the universe.

- **He is the Lord of Hosts** (Isa. 6:3,4). He is the commander of the myriads upon myriads of angelic beings, as well as commander-in-chief of every single tiny atom and molecule in the whole universe.

- **He is loving** (1 John 4:8–16). He has never stopped loving you from the day you were imagined.

We are physical beings—we have bodies. Yet it is the spirit inside our bodies that gives us emotion, life, and personality. John 6:63 tells us that "it is the Holy Spirit who gives life to the flesh." And when we surrender our lives to Christ, our spirits move from death to life. This now-alive "spirit" within us enables us to worship God in spirit and truth, meaning our now-alive spirits are completely engaged in unrestrained, wholehearted, fanatically radical worship of our Father because we know the truth about how great He is! When the truth hits us, our spirits cannot possibly keep quiet.

Final Thoughts and Questions:

- How has Father manifested Himself in these ways to you? List them. Dwell on them. Ask Him to show more of Himself to you.

- Can you add to the list by naming three other characteristics of God that are important to you?

Prayer

Father, You are such a good Father on so many levels. I worship Your name, for Your name is great and holy. Teach me more of You. Open my spiritual eyes to see You and understand You in a deeper way. I want to know You in truth, *so that my spirit can completely engage in wholly unashamed worship of You! Amen.*

Day Thirteen

YAHWEH'S Attributes

*Great are the works of the LORD; they are studied by
all who delight in them. Splendid and majestic is His work;
and His righteousness endures forever.*
—PSALM 111:2–3

ONE OF THE WAYS WE LEARN TO UNDERSTAND WHY YAHWEH
does the things He does is by searching out and meditating on His
attributes. A wonderful way to do that is by considering some of the
Hebrew names for God. They are beautiful, but besides that, they
clearly illustrate His wonderful qualities. (I based this listing of names
on Dr. Judson Cornwall and Dr. Stelman Smith's *The Exhaustive Dictionary of Bible Names*, from Thomas Nelson, published in 1998.)

- **El Shaddai**—God Almighty
- **El Rohi**—God is my Shepherd
- **El Berith**—God of the Covenants [Some of the covenants
  are Noahic (Gen. 9), Abrahamic (Gen. 17), Mosaic (Ex. 24),
  Davidic (2 Sam. 7), and Christ (Matt. 26:28).]
- **El Olam**—God of eternity
- **El Elyon**—God Most High
- **Yah**—breath
- **Yehovah Gmolah**—God of recompenses (This title speaks
  of the just nature of God against all unrighteousness. In pure
  justice, He will repay what is deserved.)
- **Yehovah Heleyon**—God the lofty one, who inhabits eternity

- **Yehovah Hoseenu**—Lord our maker
- **Yehovah Yireh**—God our provider
- **Yehovah Nissi**—The Lord of my banner (This banner is the flag we wave as we march into battle, which states that we belong to God.)
- **Yehovah Rophe**—Lord who heals
- **Yehovah Sabaoth**—Lord of hosts
- **Yehovah Shalom**—God of peace
- **Yehovah Tsidkenu**—Lord is righteousness

I love the names of the Lord. All of them. And I love His attributes. Getting to know the Father is the most important quest we could ever embark on.

In seeking to know Him better, I've learned that if God said something or did something, that settles it. End of debate. I should never doubt or question it; instead I should dig deeper to find and understand the truth behind His words and actions. And if my interpretation of His words and actions doesn't line up with Scripture, then the problem must be with my interpretation. God never violates Scripture—which is, after all, His own Word.

Anytime our understanding of God confuses us, we can always look to Jesus, whose words and actions are the most beautiful and perfect representation of God's loving heart.

Final Thoughts and Questions

When you run across characteristics of God you don't understand, write them down. Then ask Father to show you through Scripture or through His Spirit how to understand those aspects of His character that confuse you. Ask questions. Dive into your research. God likes your questions, and He loves to reveal to you the deeper truths about Himself.

Prayer

Heavenly Father, blessed be Your holy name now and forever. You are beautiful in all Your ways. You are good. You are slow to anger. You are rich in mercy. And how beautiful is Your holy Son, who shows me Your beautiful heart. Teach me more, Father. Open my eyes to more of You. Amen.

Day Fourteen

A Good Father

See how great a love the Father has bestowed on us,
that we should be called children of God; and such we are.
—1 JOHN 3:1

MY DAD IS GREAT! WHEN I WAS A CHILD, HE ASSURED ME FRE-quently that he loved me. He tickled often and patiently taught me how to downhill ski, ride a bike, and ice skate. He worked hard—sometimes at two jobs—to provide for my every need. I am blessed to be able to call my sweet papa *my* papa!

But not everyone has been blessed with an earthly father like mine. Some dads have been absent, harsh, or neglectful, and as a result many of their children grow up with a skewed idea of who God the Father really is. It's hard for the children of fathers like that to look at their heavenly Father as kind and benevolent.

This breaks my heart, and I know it breaks God's heart as well. He feels the pain of those children and longs to gather them into His arms to comfort them. God is not like those harsh fathers. In fact, Father God is far above *any* earthly fathers, even on their best days.

And it's a good thing for me that He is so good! Since I mess up on such a regular basis, I have often wondered why God loves me. And then one day God impressed this upon me: *You have children who mess up regularly, and yet you still love them and would do anything to help them. Why would I be any different?*

Yes, we are His kids. And yes, He loves us even when we mess up. There is nothing He wouldn't do to help us and save us.

When we look at our Father in this way—as our loving, endlessly patient Father—we can understand His goodness better. He blesses us beyond measure every day. We wake up every morning—a blessing from Father. We eat breakfast—a provision from Father. We kiss our kids—who are one of the greatest gifts from Father. We drive to work—a provision from Father. We relate to others and build relationships—a blessing from Papa. We can touch, we can smile, we can laugh and cry, we rejoice, we submit to and experience life—a blessing from our Papa.

The *best* gift our good Father gave is that He placed within each of us a pure and perfect soul. That gift is eternal, because He wants to be with us eternally.

God's heart is blessed when we recognize His gifts. And those gifts are all around us. We only need eyes to see them and lips that say, "Thank You for Your goodness."

Final Thoughts and Questions

Go through this day with eyes open to every blessing Father God has given you. Find them, acknowledge them, thank Papa—and repeat.

Prayer

God, You are a good Father. Open my eyes to all the blessings You pour into my life every day. And then help me, in turn, to be a good parent to my own children. Help me to follow Your good example. Amen.

Day Fifteen

Who Is Jesus?

*"She will bear a Son; and you shall call His name Jesus,
for He will save His people from their sins."*
—MATTHEW 1:21

NOW THAT WE UNDERSTAND WHO OUR BOSS IS AND WHAT HE wants from us, it's time to learn more about our Foreman—Jesus Christ. He shows us how to live out the Boss's directives, and how to do it in a way that blesses the Boss.

Jesus. His is the most famous name of all. More books have been written about Him than about anyone else who has ever lived. He is debated, misunderstood, and adored. Churches and ministries preach about Him. Many people love Him and would willingly give their lives for Him, while others belittle, ignore, and curse Him.

The Bible has more than three hundred prophecies concerning Jesus and His role as Messiah. Forty of them are specific. Here is just some of what Old Testament prophecies say the Messiah had to be:

- born of a virgin
- a descendant of Abraham
- from the tribe of Judah
- from the house of David
- born in Bethlehem
- taken to Egypt
- anointed by the Holy Spirit
- heralded by a messenger (who turned out to be John the Baptist)

In addition, the Messiah had to:
- perform miracles
- cleanse the temple
- enter Jerusalem riding on a donkey
- be rejected by His own people
- die a humiliating death, complete with betrayal by a friend

Further, the Bible prophesies that the Messiah would be:
- sold for thirty pieces of silver
- silent before accusers
- mocked, beaten, pierced, spat upon
- crucified with thieves
- given vinegar
- buried in a rich man's tomb

Despite the violence of His death, the Old Testament also says no bones would be broken. It says soldiers would cast lots for His garments. Then, it says, He would rise from the dead, ascend to heaven, and sit at the Father's right hand.

The statistical odds of one man randomly fulfilling even seven of these prophecies is staggering. The odds of one man fulfilling all three hundred of them is unfathomable—unless, of course, that man was indeed the Son of God and the promised Messiah.

Jesus's Hebrew name, the name his family called him, is Yehushua (Yeshua for short), meaning "God is salvation." Who is this Yehushua? He is the Messiah, the son of YAHWEH. He is the Word made flesh, the living Word of God, the living Torah (Law). He has been around since creation (He helped to create the world), and He is found throughout the Old Testament. Jesus (Yehushua) is the righteous right arm of the Father.

Even more, His name is like His Father's: "My name is in him" (Ex. 23:21). And like the rest of the prophecies, this one proved to be true: YAHWEH is the highest name of all. None is higher.

Final Thoughts and Questions

Jesus is the narrow gate to God. The better we get to know Him, the more our feet stay glued to the path that leads to God. The book of Hebrews paints an accurate picture of the fullness of our King and Messiah. I encourage you to read it over and over so you never abandon the way to God.

Prayer

Father, thank You for giving us Your precious Son. He is so much more than I ever imagined. Give me eyes to see more of Him. Amen.

Messiah Fulfilled the Spring Feasts of YAHWEH

Clean out the old leaven so that you may be a new lump, just as you are in fact unleavened. For Christ our Passover also has been sacrificed. Therefore let us celebrate the feast, not with old leaven, nor with the leaven of malice and wickedness, but with the unleavened bread of sincerity and truth.

—1 CORINTHIANS 5:7–8

I HAVE BEEN A CHRIST FOLLOWER FOR DECADES. ALL THAT TIME, I thought I had a full knowledge of who Christ is. But recently, I started learning about the Feasts of God (Lev. 23) and how Christ fulfilled them. My understanding of Christ deepened more than I could have ever imagined. Not only did my understanding grow, but I felt incredibly blessed—like my heart was burning within me.

I want to share them to bless you and help you know Christ deeper than you've known Him before. I'm simply describing some amazing celebrations our Savior reveled in. In fact, not only did He celebrate them, but He fulfilled them.

More accurately, Jesus has fulfilled four of the seven feasts of God and will soon fulfill the remaining three. Let's look at the four spring feasts—the feasts He has fulfilled—and learn some profound things about our Messiah.

The Feast of Passover is the first spring feast. It commemorates Moses delivering the children of Israel from their bondage of slavery in Egypt. On that long-ago night of the first Passover, Moses instructed every Hebrew family to take a ritually pure male lamb and kill it without breaking any of its bones. They then sprinkled its blood on the doorposts of their homes. When the angel of death passed through the land, He saw the blood and "passed over," thereby saving everyone inside from death.

Jesus—a perfectly pure, unbroken male—was sacrificed at the precise hour of the day the nation's Passover lamb was slaughtered during the celebration of this feast. His blood sprinkled on the doorposts of our hearts saves us from eternal death. Jesus fulfilled this feast to a *T*.

Passover marks the first day of the seven-day Feast of Unleavened Bread. During this feast, each home searches for and removes every crumb of leaven (yeast) from within its boundaries. Only flat, unleavened bread is eaten for seven days in celebration and in anticipation of the unleavened Messiah. Biblically, in most cases, leaven represents sin. Even a little leaven quickly affects a whole batch of bread. Similarly, if we deliberately leave even one sin in our lives, the results are disastrous. Jesus fulfilled this feast by being the perfect, sinless Lamb of God who takes away the sins of the world.

The Feast of First Fruits is celebrated by waving the first fruits of the barley harvest in the air before God. This feast represents all who believe and put their trust in the Messiah. Jesus fulfilled this third spring feast by rising from the grave on this day. "[Jesus is] the first-fruits of those who have fallen asleep" (1 Cor. 15:20 NIV).

The Feast of Shavuot/Pentecost occurs fifty days after Passover. This fourth spring feast commemorates the giving of the Law (God's instructions—the Torah) on Mount Sinai. Some say this feast concludes the Passover season. Jesus fulfilled this feast when He sent the Holy Spirit at Pentecost.

- **On Shavuot:** The commandments were written on stone by the finger of God on top of Mount Sinai. That day three thousand people died because of their rebellion against God's commands (Ex. 32:28).

- **On Pentecost:** The commandments were written on people's hearts by the Spirit of God on Mount Zion. That day three thousand people were filled with God's Spirit (Acts 2:41). Jesus fulfilled this feast by ascending into heaven and sending the Holy Spirit to earth to comfort and guide believers.

Final Thoughts and Questions

Because Jesus is your mediator, the one who represents you before Father, I believe it is of great importance that you know as much about Him as you possibly can. Studying these feasts of God is a great way to know Him in a deeper sense. I encourage you to read the following Scriptures, take notes, and look for shadows of the Messiah in each feast.

- **Passover:** Exodus 3:1–12:13
- **Unleavened Bread:** Exodus 12:13–51
- **Firstfruits:** Exodus 13; Leviticus 23:10–22
- **Shavuot:** Exodus 19–20
- **Pentecost:** Acts 2

Prayer

Father, Your plan of redemption is seen in the whole Bible. Help me, as I study Your feasts, to see Your Son and Your great plan of redemption throughout every feast. I want to know Your Son better. Amen.

Messiah Will Fulfill the Fall Feasts of YAHWEH

Nehemiah, who was the governor, and Ezra the priest and scribe,
and the Levites who taught the people said to all the people,
"This day is holy to the LORD your God; do not mourn or weep."
For all the people were weeping when they heard the words of the
law. Then he said to them, "Go, eat of the fat, drink of the sweet,
and send portions to him who has nothing prepared;
for this day is holy to our Lord. Do not be grieved,
for the joy of the LORD is your strength."
—NEHEMIAH 8:9–10

AFTER SEVENTY YEARS OF CAPTIVITY IN BABYLON, THE ISRAELITES were finally able to return to Jerusalem and rebuild the walls. They rejoiced when Nehemiah read the words of the Law aloud. They rejoiced over the restoration of the feasts of God. They wept with repentant hearts over their abandonment of the feasts, but Nehemiah told them, "Rejoice, for this day is holy."

Like the returned captives, I rejoiced when I learned about the feasts. I too recognized them as deep spiritual treasures. I recognized the Messiah in each one and delighted in them.

The fall feasts of God are not only treasures, they are futuristic, yet to be fulfilled. They give us insights into our Messiah and His role toward us on earth in these final days. In fact, if we want to fully understand the last days, we must first study the fall feasts of God.

The Feast of Trumpets/Rosh Hashanah (Yom Teruah). This is the first of the fall feasts. The day starts the Ten Days of Awe—ten days of preparing one's soul to stand before the One True God on judgment day. Ten days of spiritual introspection. Ten days of seeking forgiveness and making restitution for sins. It marks the time when God opens His books (see Rev. 20:12). Jesus will fulfill this feast when He returns with a blast of the trumpet (shofar) and takes us to His kingdom.

The Day of Atonement (Yom Kippur). This feast is the holiest day of the year, a day of soul searching and praying. It represents the great white throne judgment day. Jesus will fulfill this feast by sitting at God's right hand on judgment day, where He will plead our case for us. Only through Jesus's blood can we be found not guilty when we stand before YAHWEH.

At sundown, on the closing of this day, it is said that the books are closed. Our scapegoat—Yehushua the Messiah (Lev. 16:5–10)—has taken the sins of all humankind upon Himself, cleansing us of our sins and redeeming us back to Father. Because of Him, our names are written and sealed in the Lamb's Book of Life.

The Feast of Booths or Feast of Tabernacles (Sukkot). This feast too represents events of the future: the thousand-year period when Jesus will rule and reign from the new Jerusalem. It is symbolic of how God will "tabernacle" with His people, as He did during the Israelites' exodus from Egypt.

The last days are closing in on us. But as we study the fall feasts, we should not be filled with dread. Instead, because of Jesus, our hearts should rejoice. Our sins are forgiven. The Spirit of God lives within us. Our names are written in the Lamb's Book of Life. We get to rule and reign with Christ for a thousand years. We have the privilege and honor of living in Father's kingdom forever. What a blessing!

Jesus is our promised Messiah. God has given us clues and pictures of Him since the beginning of time, and Jesus fulfilled each one perfectly. What a beautiful and loving God we have to point us in the right direction. What a beautiful and loving Savior He gave us. Hallelujah!

Final Thoughts and Questions

As you did for the spring feasts, study the Scriptures (Lev. 23:24–44) that describe the fall feasts—the Feast of Trumpets, Yom Kippur, and the Feast of Tabernacles. Take notes and search for the foreshadowing of the Messiah.

Prayer

Father, thank You for the fall feasts. They help me to understand Christ more profoundly. They point the way to the Messiah and give me a great hope for a future with You and Your Son. Open my eyes to see Your Son in the fall feasts. Amen.

All That Messiah Has Done

*[Jesus] is the radiance of [God's] glory
and the exact representation of His nature,
and upholds all things by the word of His power.
When He had made purification of sins,
He sat down at the right hand of the Majesty on high,
having become as much better than the angels,
as He has inherited a more excellent name than they.*
—HEBREWS 1:3–4

KNOWLEDGE OF GOD'S CHARACTER LETS US WORSHIP HIM IN SPIRIT and truth (see day 13), because the truths of His nature help us worship Him with greater devotion and zeal. We know Him better, so we can worship Him more fully. The same is true with Christ. When we know Him better, our praise and adoration come from a heart and spirit full of love because we understand truths about His nature better.

So far, we have understood that Christ fulfilled over three hundred prophecies, and we have detected his behind-the-scenes presence throughout the Old Testament and throughout God's feasts. Now let's search out more of what He has done for us and all that He is.

Chapter 1 in the book of Hebrews keeps a running list of Christ's messiahship merits:

- Verse 2 says Christ is heir of all things. The world was made through Him.

- Verse 3 says He is the radiance of God's glory, the exact representation of God's nature. He upholds the entire world by the power of His Word. He is made a purification of sins. He is seated on the right hand of the Majesty on high.

- Verse 4 says He is superior to angels. His name is superior to theirs.

- Verse 6 says all angels worship him.

- Verse 8 says His throne is "forever and ever, and the righteous scepter is the scepter of His kingdom."

- Verse 9 says He loves righteousness and hates lawlessness. God anointed Him with the oil of gladness.

- Verse 13 says He sits at God's right hand until all enemies are made a footstool under His feet.

The book of Hebrews paints a picture of the Levitical high priesthood, whose role was to mediate between a holy God and an unholy people; it was a priesthood that needed the sprinkling of blood for the remission of sin. The Levitical priesthood foreshadowed Christ as our perfect High Priest. Hebrews 4:15 says, "For we do not have a high priest who cannot sympathize with our weaknesses, but One who has been tempted in all things as we are, yet without sin."

With these characteristics in mind, how can we not adore Him? He is so good. And what makes Him even more awesome is that Christ shows us Father's heart. He is the perfect example of our Papa!

Final Thoughts and Questions

I encourage you to read the whole book of Hebrews. It paints a true picture of who our Redeemer is and what His role is to mankind. Create a list of all Christ's merits. Then, since Christ shows us Father's heart, connect those qualities to Father. For example, if Christ is unchanging, how has God proven His unchanging nature?

Prayer

Jesus, thank You for being my superior High Priest. Thank You for Your blood that was sprinkled on the heavenly mercy seat for the remission of my sins. I will never take that blood for granted. I love You. Amen.

Day Nineteen

True Discipleship

Take My yoke upon you and learn from Me,
for I am gentle and humble in heart,
and you will find rest for your souls.
—MATTHEW 11:29

IF YOU HAD ASKED ME FIVE YEARS AGO WHAT DISCIPLESHIP MEANS, I could not have given you a complete answer. I probably would have said something vague, like "It means you follow Jesus" or "It means being a good person."

Discipleship is one of those Christian buzzwords many believers have never been able to fully comprehend.

To understand, I had to go back to first-century Israel and follow Christ around a bit to observe His disciples in action. This is what I discovered: Christ's disciples gave up everything familiar and comfortable to follow Him. They listened to and memorized His words, some even writing them down so they could accurately share His message with others. They altered their old way of thinking so even their thoughts would resemble their teacher's. They modified their actions so they would act like their teacher. In short, they tried to imitate their teacher in every aspect of life. They tried to become mirror images of Him.

This is what is required of you and me if we want to become true disciples of Jesus. We need to alter our thinking, attitudes, actions, responses, patterns of forgiveness, and our willingness to be servants. With the Holy Spirit's help, we need to transform our image into the image of Christ so that we too become mirror images of Him.

This takes a lot of work. A complete dying of self; becoming last, least, and a servant to all. But Christ showed us how. He gave up His beautiful home where everything is perfect and holy to come here to earth where everything is fallen and sinful. He gave up His life so we could live. He was completely obedient to His Father's plan—even though that plan included pain and suffering and rejection.

Christ showed us how to love. He showed us how to overcome temptation. He showed us how to forgive. He is our perfect example of everything.

When I began to understand this concept, my life completely changed. I knew I had to start monitoring my actions, reactions, thoughts, and attitudes to change them into Christlike thoughts, actions, reactions, and attitudes. I knew it would be a huge struggle to create change, but I also knew the rewards would be eternal. I haven't looked back since that day, because the blessings are powerful. I invite you, dear friend, to do the same. Join me on this discipleship journey, and we will learn and grow and remodel our spiritual lives together.

Final Thoughts and Questions

Ponder this question today: Are you ready to be a true disciple? It requires your all! Once you start, you can't look back. You can't quit. Too much is at stake.

Prayer

Father, help me to live as a true disciple, a mirror image of Your perfect, holy Son. Open my spiritual eyes to see areas in my life where I have fallen short of His image. Give me strength and wisdom to make changes today. Amen.

Day Twenty

Think Like Messiah

For who has known the mind of the Lord, that he will instruct Him? But we have the mind of Christ.
—1 CORINTHIANS 2:16

OUR THOUGHTS CAN GET US INTO TROUBLE—FAST.

Shopping for groceries one day—a tedious duty that drains me on so many levels—I finally head to checkout. With a great sigh of relief, I'm about to take my place in line when out of nowhere a loud and somewhat obnoxious family walks right in front of me and rudely cuts me off. I can feel my teeth clench and my eyes widen, but since I was raised to be polite, I just smile at them—with crazy eyes. But *in my head* I'm saying some ugly things. *In my head* I criticize their weight, their haircuts, and I even call their baby ugly (which I really didn't mean, because I love all babies).

The Holy Spirit admonished me right then and there by pointing out *my* ugliness. He reminded me that even if I didn't say all that, thinking it was still wrong! It's not good enough to *not* say the bad things; He wants me to not even think the bad things, because what's going on in my head will eventually come out in negative actions or words.

I was somber on my ride home. I felt small and sheepish, like a kid caught with her hand in the cookie jar. But I felt repentant as well. I really do want to be a better disciple.

When we are His disciples, Christ is concerned with the thoughts we entertain. He wants our minds pure—as His mind is pure. He wants our thoughts to be a mirror image of His.

According to the research funded by the National Science Foundation, we humans have somewhere between fifty thousand and seventy thousand thoughts per day. That's thirty-five to forty-eight thoughts per minute, or a thought every 1.7 seconds. Each of those thoughts has the potential to either help in the pursuit of purity or cause impurity. Every thought should be either nurtured and explored or expelled and banished.

When I got home from my shopping trip still feeling convicted, I knew I had to make a change. I decided to put a filter on my thoughts—all fifty thousand of them. I became far more conscious of my thoughts by asking myself, *Are these thoughts Christlike? Should I keep them or get rid of them? Would Christ think thoughts like these?*

This filter works! It continues to help me conquer my thought life. It helps me look more like Christ—from the inside out. It helps me be a better disciple. It helps me improve my attitudes toward my family. It helps me create a better environment in my marriage. It quite literally has changed and continues to change my life.

Final Thoughts and Questions

I encourage you to get your brain fitted with a Jesus filter. Start by listening to your thoughts. What are they saying? Are they thoughts Christ would think? If they don't sound like Christ, then get rid of them. Repent of them and ask the Holy Spirit to help you think like Christ.

What kinds of thoughts do you think Christ thought? Start writing them down. Start transforming your brain.

Prayer

Father, help my thoughts be like Christ's thoughts today:

- *compassionate*
- *selfless*
- *kind*
- *aware of my fingerprint on every soul*
- *considerate*
- *fair*
- *nonjudgmental*
- *merciful*
- *patient*
- *obedient*

Day Twenty-One

Be Like Messiah

"Everyone who hears these words
of Mine and acts on them,
may be compared to a wise man
who built his house on the rock."
—MATTHEW 7:24

WE ALL HAVE CERTAIN AREAS THAT CHALLENGE US MORE THAN others. We think we're being good disciples, but when that "certain thing" pops up, we blow it. One of those areas of special challenge for me is teasing. I can accept teasing from everyone but my husband. His teasing instantly raises my defenses, turning me into someone scary and ugly—resembling a she-wolf.

Once, when he was somewhat lovingly teasing me, I took a swing at him. That's right—I tried to punch him! At which he laughed. This, of course, made me want to hurt him more. I'm not proud of this, and I assure you I haven't swung a fist at my dear husband for a long time. But his teasing *still* ticks me off. Why? I couldn't tell you—but I did know my response to it had to change. This instinct had to become more Christlike, less Mary-like. I knew my actions and reactions needed to resemble Christ, and for me this would require much, much, much change.

In my discipleship journey I have observed that once my thoughts start to transform, my actions are next in line. That means I had to stop throwing right hooks at people who tick me off. And when I put a "Christ filter" on my actions, change *did* happen. I began to look at my marriage and ask myself, *Do I serve my spouse in the areas where he needs me to serve? Do I respect him? Am I a good helpmate? Do I serve him in the bedroom? Do I spend time connecting with him?*

I also put the Christ filter on my interactions with my children. I asked myself, *Am I respecting my children, or am I manipulating them? Are my words encouraging or destroying? Am I showing my love? Do I serve them with a smile and a prayer?*

I put the filter on when I interacted with humanity. I asked myself, *Do I treat others as if they are God's children? Do I show God I love Him by loving those whom He made? Am I honoring or dishonoring? Am I rude or kind?*

I put the filter on my everyday life and asked, *Am I following the commandments as Christ did? Do I lie or gossip? Am I full of greed and lust? Do I honor and love those around me? Do I reach out to the hurting? Am I content with being the last, or do I push my way to the front? Am I going the extra mile without grouching about it? Am I turning the other cheek? Am I doing small acts of kindness—in secret, without tooting my own horn?*

Just like my decision to be like Christ with my thoughts, I decided to be like Christ with my actions. I wanted to be like Jesus in every single area of my life.

And I must say, nothing has been more challenging. Every single, itty-bitty, tiny little compartment of my life is challenged. Everything in my life is in the process of being spiritually remodeled. And nothing has helped me to make that change more than this Christ filter. It really does help me filter out my sin-driven selfishness, to become more Christlike in everything. Every day the filter catches something, and I am confronted to change it.

Christ calls us to "be perfect like my Father is perfect" (Matt. 5:48, paraphrased). Jesus is the perfect representation of the Father's heart, which makes Him the perfect example to follow in our perfection journey.

Final Thoughts and Questions

When you trust Jesus and follow Him in every single area of your life, He ensures your feet stay solidly on the narrow path that leads to God. But remember, first it is a decision, then it is action—an action that demands all!

How are your actions? I'm sure you, like me, sometimes react in a way you aren't proud of. What are the things that cause those reactions in you? List them, and then make the decision to put a Christ filter on your actions. Make that decision to be like Jesus today.

Prayer

Father, help my actions to resemble Your Son's actions. Help me to be loving, kind, and thoughtful. Help me to see others as You see them—as Your children. Help me to love as Your Son loved. Amen.

Forgive Like Messiah

Love your enemies, and do good,
and lend, expecting nothing in return;
and your reward will be great.
—LUKE 6:35

SOMEONE IN MY LIFE HAS CAUSED ME GREAT SUFFERING.
One night I had a vivid dream. I was back in the house where I grew up. I was not alone—demons of every type were there. Objects were floating around, things were thrown at me, and I was scared! I tried to leave the house by the front door, but every time I tried to leave, the demons grabbed my ankles and pulled me back in.

I woke up very upset, kicking my legs like a wild woman. And I knew the dream had been more than a dream; it had a spiritual meaning. I asked Father what it meant. This is what I felt Him say:

The house represents the life of the one who has caused you such pain. Spiritual forces are keeping that person trapped inside their mode of operation. Every time they try to leave their way of life and make an improvement, evil forces grab them and pull them back in.

I felt as if the Holy Spirit was telling me I needed to pray for this person, praying for victory over the evil holding them in, and for spiritual freedom.

The thing is, I didn't *want* to pray for their freedom. I wanted this person to suffer. But after several days of fighting the Holy Spirit about it, I was convicted. I repented of my unforgiving attitude and started praying for this person. I'm still praying. No change has occurred in this person's life yet, but I will not stop praying.

Christ taught us how to forgive. While the Roman soldiers were in the very act of pounding spikes into his wrists and ankles, he prayed, "Father, forgive them; for they do not know what they are doing" (Luke 23:34). Wow!

The example He set for us in that scene is that we should pray for our enemies. He is so wise; He knew when we pray for our enemies, forgiveness comes easier. He knew prayer chases out the bitterness and cleans our spiritual house. He knew forgiveness coupled with prayer breaks all chains and sets us spiritually free.

His way is always best—for you, for me, and for all mankind.

Final Thoughts and Questions

In the same measure you forgive, you will be forgiven—by the Great Judge on judgment day. It's important that we learn to forgive Christ's way *now*, before it's too late. How are you at forgiving others? Be set free from unforgiveness today by purposing to forgive those who have sinned against you. Then seal the deal by praying for your offender. This is how we forgive like Christ.

Prayer

Father, I want to forgive as Christ forgave. I want to pray for my enemies as Christ did. So in my heart I purpose to forgive anyone and everyone who has ever hurt me. Bring these people to my mind so I can pray for their redemption and spiritual well-being. Amen.

Serve Like Messiah

*"Whoever wishes to become great among you
shall be your servant."*
—MATTHEW 20:26

ABOVE ALL ELSE, CHRIST WAS A SERVANT. IN THIS, ONCE AGAIN, HE led by example. He healed the sick, He bound the wounds of the brokenhearted, He fed the hungry—both physically and spiritually—and in the greatest act of service of all, He gave His own life so we could live.

And let's not be naive. His constant serving probably wore Him out. He often tried to get away from the crowds so He could talk to His Abba and get reenergized. But the crowds always found Him and pulled Him back in, which he allowed and even encouraged. Bottom line, He loved us and showed us how much He did by serving us unconditionally.

He calls us to serve unconditionally as well, even though it's hard and drains us emotionally, physically, and spiritually. He wants us to follow His example and serve willingly, even with joy.

Final Thoughts and Questions

Serving like Christ is never easy. But if you're serious about discipleship, then serve you must. How have you been at serving others in the past? How can you be a better servant today at home, at work, at school?

I started to make this principle a part of my life by serving those closest to me: my own family—my spouse, my kids, my in-laws, my siblings, my parents—and my friends.

I asked myself, *What act of love does my spouse need me to fulfill for him today? What do my kids need from me that will bless their socks off— and even point them to Christ? How can I serve my siblings, or parents, or in-laws today?*

We all have needs and desires that only those closest to us can fulfill. What are yours? What do you think your family's needs and wishes are? I suggest making a list. I did, and it has helped me identify and meet needs I otherwise would never have thought about.

This one thought keeps me serving with a smile: *When I serve others, I am also serving God.*

Prayer

Father, thank You for the example of servanthood Your Son so flawlessly showed mankind. I want to serve as He did. Please show me how. Open my eyes to the needs of those around me, and give me the strength and courage to meet those needs by serving. Amen.

Resist Temptation Like Messiah

Let no one say when he is tempted, "I am being tempted by God,"
for God cannot be tempted by evil, and He Himself
does not tempt anyone. But each one is tempted
when he is carried away and enticed
by his own lust. Then when lust has conceived,
it gives birth to sin; and when sin is accomplished,
it brings forth death. Do not be deceived, my beloved brethren.
Every good thing given and every perfect gift is from above,
coming down from the Father of lights,
with whom there is no variation or shifting shadow.
—JAMES 1:13–17

WE ALL FACE TEMPTATION. NO ONE IS EXEMPT. WHETHER THE temptation walks on two legs or sits in a bowl covered in chocolate sauce, temptations pull at us all. Christ was no different. He too was tempted. But what is more important is that He defeated His temptations. And by doing so, He showed us how we can too.

Immediately after His baptism by John, Christ went to the wilderness to fast and pray before He started His official ministry. For forty long days and probably even longer nights, Jesus went without food. In His weakened state, the Enemy came to tempt Him.

- **Temptation 1:** "If You are the Son of God, command this stone to become bread" (Luke 4:3 NKJV). Satan is not only tempting a hungry man, he is also trying to plant seeds of doubt in Christ's mind, questioning His messiahship. But Christ used Scripture to defeat His foe. He quoted from Deuteronomy 8:3: "It is written, 'Man shall not live by bread alone, but by every word that proceeds from the mouth of God'" (Matt. 4:4 NKJV).

- **Temptation 2:** Satan then showed Jesus all the kingdoms of the world. He said, "I will give You all this domain and its glory; for it has been handed over to me, and I give it to whomever I wish. Therefore if You worship before me, it shall all be Yours" (Luke 4:6–7). Once again Satan was trying to plant seeds of doubt in Christ's mind about His messiahship, and he was trying to get Christ to take the easy way out: *Instead of going to the cross, worship me and I will give it all to you.* But Christ would have none of it, and instead quoted from Deuteronomy 6:13, "You shall worship the Lord your God and serve Him only" (Luke 4:8).

- **Temptation 3:** Satan took Jesus to the pinnacle of the temple in Jerusalem and said, "If You are the Son of God, throw Yourself down from here; for it is written, 'He will command His angels concerning You to guard You'" (Luke 4:9–10). The Enemy was trying to manipulate Jesus to manipulate God—*Jump and God will be forced to send His angels to protect you.* This temptation must have been incredibly strong for Christ, because it would have given Him instant credibility with the Jews—the Messiah coming down from above on the wings of angels. But Christ did not give in. Instead He quoted from Deuteronomy 6:16, "You shall not put the Lord Your God to the test" (Luke 4:12).

Final Thoughts and Questions

Christ used Scripture to defeat temptation's powerful lure. You can too. Whatever is tempting you today, Scriptures deal with it. Let's be like Christ. Let's use Scripture to defeat the Enemy and send him packing.

If your temptation is

- gossip, use Proverbs 20:19 and Psalm 34:13.
- lying, use Proverbs 12:22 and Leviticus 19:11.
- adultery, use Proverbs 6:32 and Matthew 5:28.
- pornography, use Matthew 5:28.
- anger, use James 1:19–20 and Proverbs 29:11.
- materialism, use 1 Timothy 6:7–8, Ecclesiastes 5:10, and Matthew 6:11.
- overeating, use 1 Corinthians 10:31 and Proverbs 23:2.

Prayer

Father, thank You for giving me a way out of every temptation that tries to snare me. Thank You for Christ, who shows me how to do battle against the Enemy. Send Your Holy Spirit to give me strength to fight temptation, and bring to my attention Scriptures that will help me do battle against it. Amen.

Day Twenty-Five

Trust in Jesus— the True Messiah

[Jesus] was asking His disciples, "Who do people say that the Son
of Man is?" And they said, "Some say John the Baptist; and others,
Elijah; but still others, Jeremiah, or one of the prophets."
He said to them, "But who do you say that I am?" Simon Peter
answered, "You are the Christ, the Son of the living God."
—MATTHEW 16:13–16

I RECENTLY FOUND A BLOG THAT SHARES INSIGHTS INTO THE CUL-
ture and thoughts of first-century Israel. The author investigates what
the common people were waiting and watching for with great anticipation and zeal.

Daniel prophesied in Daniel 9:25, "So you are to know and discern that *from the issuing of a decree to restore and rebuild Jerusalem*
until Messiah the Prince there will be seven weeks and sixty-two weeks"
(emphasis mine). Because this prophecy reveals the exact year the
Messiah would ascend through the clouds and onto His heavenly
throne (AD 33), many men were trying to claim the "messiah" title.
The Pharisees, who were well aware of this prophecy, distinguished
two categories of miracles: *common miracles* and *Messianic miracles*
(miracles only the true Messiah could perform). They did this so they
would be able to clearly recognize the true Messiah when he appeared.

Here are what the Pharisees called Messianic miracles:

Healing a Jewish leper. Historical accounts indicate that leprosy was
considered a punishment from God for sins committed. The Pharisees

91

reasoned that only God could forgive sins, so only the true Messiah would be able to perform this type of miracle.

Christ healed a Jewish leper in Mark 1:40–45.

Casting out a mute demon. Because the rabbis had the spiritual authority to cast out demons, they would go to the possessed and ask the demon its name. Once the demon answered with its name, the rabbis would be able to cast it out. Only the true Messiah would know a demon's name without asking it.

In Matthew 12:22–23, Christ casts the demon out of the mute man.

Healing of a man born blind. The rabbis believed being born blind was a curse from the Almighty and that only God could remove a curse.

Christ performed His third Messianic miracle in John 9:1–7 when He opened the eyes of a man blind since birth.

Raising a dead man after four days. When a person died, it was believed, his or her spirit would stay close to the body for three days.

In John 11:1–44, Christ raised Lazarus, who had been dead for four days. For someone to be raised after four days was truly a messianic miracle. After this miracle, the people were truly astounded and many believed in Him.

This, to me, is proof the world needs to hear. We have prophetic proof, we have historic proof, and we have eyewitnesses who saw Jesus ascend through the clouds to heaven. These proofs burn in my heart. They offer all the proof I need to know that when I follow Christ, I am on that narrow path to God.

Final Thoughts and Questions

You can trust Jesus. You can trust that He shows you the only way to God. You can trust that when you live as He lived, you are pleasing the Father and building His kingdom here on earth.

How are your trust levels in Christ? Do you believe He is the true Messiah—the only Son of the living God?

Prayer

Father, Your Son is beautiful in every way. I love Him with all my heart. I know beyond a shadow of a doubt that I can trust Him with my life. I can trust Him to show me how to live. I can trust Him with my everything. Amen.

Apprentice
under the Holy Spirit

To be transformed into Christ's likeness, we need the help of the Holy Spirit. The Holy Spirit is a great teacher. His tutelage is gentle, thorough, and powerful. Through Him we can do mighty things.

Day Twenty-Six

The Holy Spirit

A shoot will spring from the stem of Jesse, and a branch from his roots will bear fruit. The Spirit of the LORD will rest on Him, the spirit of wisdom and understanding, the spirit of counsel and strength, the spirit of knowledge and the fear of the LORD.
—ISAIAH 11:1–2

THE HOLY SPIRIT IS A MYSTERIOUS POWER. THE CHURCH IS FULL OF controversy concerning who the Holy Spirit is and how He relates to us. That's why I'd like to ignore formal religion for a moment and look directly to Christ. What did He say about the Holy Spirit, and how did the Holy Spirit lead and empower Him?

I started by reading through the book of Matthew and compiling a list of the mighty things the Holy Spirit did to help Christ.

- Immediately after Christ's baptism, the Holy Spirit helped Him fight against temptation (Matt. 4:1–11).

- The Holy Spirit empowered His preaching and teaching— fulfilling the prophecy of Isaiah 9:2, "The people who walk in darkness will see a great light."

- We know from Luke 4:14–19 that the power of the Holy Spirit helped Him preach the gospel, release the captives, heal the sick, raise the dead, cast out demons, and show the people God's true heart and point toward His kingdom.

- The Holy Spirit authenticated Christ's ministry and His fulfillment of ancient prophecy with amazing signs and wonders wherever Christ went.

Some of the sages of old say the Holy Spirit emulates all the feminine sides of God's nature: edifying, nurturing, teaching, leading, encouraging, and comforting. I love that.

Christ was empowered with six specific facets of the Holy Spirit for His ministry here on earth: "The spirit of wisdom and understanding, the spirit of counsel and strength, the spirit of knowledge and the fear of the LORD" (Isa. 11:2). If Christ was empowered with these spirits so He could fulfill His mission, then how much more do we need them in our lives today to fulfill the call He has placed on each one of us?

We need to have ears to hear the Spirit speak. We need hearts willing and obedient to do what He wants. But if you are anything like me, sometimes it's difficult to be obedient.

Many times I have heard the Holy Spirit's voice leading me in a particular direction, yet I ignored His wisdom and guidance and did what "felt right." Later, as I sat staring at disaster, I realized my feelings had misled me once again.

Have you ever done that? Many of us have. Or we sense the Holy Spirit's direction but don't like where it is headed, so we get someone else's emotionally driven advice—someone who will tell us what we want to hear—and then do whatever we wanted to do in the first place. And disaster follows.

Whatever reason we have for not asking for *and* obeying the Holy Spirit's advice, it is wrong. We need to rely on the Spirit of God as if He were God's GPS installed in our hearts. A God GPS that leads us directly to the spiritual job site. We can't ignore it or second-guess it; we need to keep it turned on and follow its directions at all times. We can't build God's perfect kingdom here on earth alone; we desperately need the Holy Spirit of God to help us.

Final Thoughts and Questions

Do you need the Holy Spirit's help today? Do you need comfort, encouragement, or direction? Go ahead and ask the Holy Spirit for His help. Then tune your ears to Him today and see and hear how He is working in your circumstances to bring about change.

Prayer

Father, help me to hear the voice of Your Spirit leading me.
Help me to be obedient and willing to go where the Spirit directs.
Help me to have a willing heart to learn Your deeper truths.
Open my spiritual eyes to see and my spiritual ears to hear Your Spirit. Amen.

The Spirit of Wisdom and Counsel

"I will ask the Father, and He will give you another Helper,
that He may be with you forever; that is the Spirit of truth,
whom the world cannot receive, because it does not see
Him or know Him, but you know Him
because He abides with you and will be in you."
—JOHN 14:16–17

WISDOM AND COUNSEL FLOW TWO WAYS—WE RECEIVE COUNSEL and we are often called upon to give counsel.

Once a dear friend of mine was struggling with a deep, hurtful issue. I listened to her and then mulled her challenge over and over in my head. Many months later, the issue was far from resolved—in fact, it was getting worse. Because I was so emotionally involved, it was hard for me to step back and give good *godly* counsel. In fact, I gave her horrible, emotionally based, namby-pamby counsel. I told her, "God wants you to be happy, so do what makes you happy." *Ugh!*

My hope was to contribute to my friend's happiness, but instead my horrible advice led to much *unhappiness!* In fact, she and I are still both reaping the terrible fruit of my advice in several areas of our lives. I'd love to have a *do over*—to go back and wrest those ill-fated words away. But I can't. I can only move forward and learn from my mistakes.

One lesson learned is that I am not so quick to give my counsel anymore. I have become a bit more careful. Would I like to be able to offer good, solid, godly counsel? Of course; that's something I hope to mature into. But before I can give good counsel, wisdom must come first. God's wisdom. His wisdom comes directly from His throne. But we need to be aware and wary of another kind of wisdom: carnal wisdom. Not surprisingly, the two kinds of wisdom often contradict each other.

Carnal wisdom is fleshly, pride-based, human reasoning. It relies on our own abilities, strengths, and senses. It does not consider the spiritual side of an issue; in fact, it is blind to spirituality. Carnal wisdom brought about the first sin. Satan told Eve, "You surely will not die [if you eat from this tree]" (Gen. 3:4). She chose to believe him—and chose to eat. She did not die *physically* on the spot, but she died *spiritually*.

As disciples of the King, we need to be on guard against using carnal wisdom as we go through life. A good way to test any "wisdom" we receive from others is to ask, *Does it line up with Scripture?* Godly wisdom always will. We must always be aware of the spiritual aspect of every issue, every problem, and every temptation. We must remember a lot more is always going on than what our dim eyes can see, so we must live by godly wisdom.

I want to be fluent in wisdom; I want to be able to offer good counsel. But getting there is a process that takes time. I believe Father wants us all to mature to that point. Godly counsel is much needed in our hurting, broken world, and wisdom is needed at every level of society. Carnality and following our own ways are leading many souls to death. "There is a way which seems right to a man, but its end is the way of death" (Prov. 16:25).

Besides giving counsel, we often need to seek counsel. When I seek counsel, I look for it conscientiously, and I look in several places. The best place is the Bible. I dig into it and search for its truths by embracing the context in which they were written. (I can get myself into trouble quickly when I slap my own emotionally driven interpretations on Bible verses.)

Godly counsel also comes from Father's voice; therefore I must be sensitive enough to hear His still, small whispers. I usually must tune out all the other loud advice and settle into stillness before I can hear His voice. Sometimes I must wait until the bitter end before I can hear Him. But He always comes through.

Godly advice can also come from trustworthy human sources, but their advice must always line up with the Word of God. It must always go through the Bible filter. If it doesn't align, then I need to keep on seeking—elsewhere.

Prayer

Father, help me to operate in the Spirit of wisdom and counsel. Fill me with Your Spirit and release the fullness of all that You have for me. Give me ears to hear Your wisdom and opportunities to share Your wise counsel. I love You. Amen.

Day Twenty-Eight

The Spirit of Knowledge and Understanding

The fear of the LORD is the beginning of wisdom,
and the knowledge of the Holy One is understanding.
—PROVERBS 9:10

I RECENTLY MADE A HUGE MISTAKE—SEVERAL HUNDRED DOLLARS' worth of mistake. A meat salesman came to my house and told me a bunch of lies to try to manipulate me into buying his meat. I took the hook, swallowed the bait, and he reeled me in for the sucker I was. I *so* regret that meat purchase, but in the moment I made the decision, I felt rushed and pressured into buying. If I had slowed down and prayed for direction and knowledge, I would have spit out the hook and sent the salesman packing. But as it was, I lacked knowledge, understanding, and the *guts* to say no!

After I'd already made the purchase, and when the foolishness of my decision was settling in, I decided to research that meat company. I found many terrible online reviews and stories that resembled mine—high-pressure sales, lies, and manipulation. To make matters worse, the meat tasted like "mystery meat Monday." Not good!

I played the *if only* game over and over in my head for days. *If only* I had told him I needed time to think over the purchase. *If only* I had taken the time to research the company. *If only* I had told him to come back in a couple of days. *If only* I had said no. How foolish I felt once I understood what kind of company his was.

The dictionary defines *understanding* as "the faculty of reasoning, discernment, and intelligence." Even more so, Job, whom I feel like I know personally, tells us in Job 28:28, "To depart from evil is understanding."

How do we get understanding? Proverbs 2:1–5 says, "My son [or daughter], if you will receive my words and treasure my commandments within you, make your ear attentive to wisdom, incline your heart to understanding; for if you cry for discernment, lift your voice for understanding; if you seek her as silver and search for her as for hidden treasures; then you will discern the fear of the LORD and discover the knowledge of God."

Why do we need understanding and knowledge? Proverbs 2:10–12 says, "For wisdom will enter your heart and knowledge will be pleasant to your soul; *discretion will guard you, understanding will watch over you, to deliver you* from the way of evil, from the man who speaks perverse things" (emphasis mine).

That meat salesman never would have gotten past me if I had listened to the Holy Spirit, who was trying desperately to get my attention that day. As I listened to the salesman, I felt uneasy—big clue #1 that the Holy Spirit was saying no! I felt rushed—another big clue telling me, *Don't do it!*

If I had been listening to the spirit of knowledge and understanding, I would have been delivered from the salesman who speaks perverse things. Next time, I will listen!

Final Thoughts and Questions

Are you seeking knowledge and understanding in any areas of your life? What are they? I encourage you to ask the Holy Spirit to give you what you seek.

Prayer

Father, I receive Your words and treasure Your commandments. I listen for wisdom and incline my heart to understanding. Fill me with the spirit of understanding and knowledge, and deliver me from the way of evil, and from any person who speaks perverse things. Amen.

The Spirit of the Fear of YAHWEH

*"Do not fear those who kill the body
but are unable to kill the soul; but rather fear Him
who is able to destroy both soul and body in hell."*
—MATTHEW 10:28

THE IDEA OF FEARING GOD—YAHWEH—ALWAYS THREW ME off-kilter. People told me it doesn't really mean *fear* Him, but more like respect Him with a holy reverence. I like that explanation, but I have still always felt it wasn't quite hitting the nail on the head.

A few years ago my family and I began observing the holy feasts of YAHWEH. It was while we celebrated our first Yom Kippur service that this whole "fear YAHWEH" idea was finally settled in my spirit. I finally understood what fearing God meant.

The Feast of Yom Kippur is like a dress rehearsal for the great white throne judgment day. On the *real* judgment day, I'm sure we will all be trembling, somber, and repentant. We will be trying to remember every single sin we committed—intentionally or unintentionally—every evil thought we entertained, every snub, every gossip, every disobedient act. We will be racking our brains to remember everything so we can repent of it. The thought that the accuser could use our unconfessed sins against us is quite a motivator toward confession and repentance.

Fear will grip our souls. God's books will be opened—our lives will be examined. Then we'll remember our Messiah. His blood covers all our confessed sin. Fear of complete spiritual destruction will dissipate, but we'll find our knees knocking just the same. The Great Judge and Eternal One calls our name. He reads our deeds, our thoughts, our everything—and He judges them.

To me, this type of fear of YAHWEH was missing from my life for too many years. For my sake, I needed to know and experience it, and celebrating Yom Kippur provided that opportunity. Fearing God has many facets. Terror, yes—but mixed with awe, respect, piety, and reverence.

Fear creates a physical response: paralysis, clenched teeth, upset stomach. It is emotional, for sure. But fear can also create a spiritual response—change, repentance, a teachable heart, and an intense respect for the One we fear.

Fear—holy fear—strengthens our spiritual foundation and humbles us before our great and mighty God, the God of the entire universe. Fear of YAHWEH promotes instant obedience to whatever He says—even when it doesn't make sense to us, even when it causes us pain, even when we don't see the benefits of it. Fear of YAHWEH creates obedience until the thing is accomplished. Abraham and Moses are great examples of people who learned to fear their Creator. And because of it, they were considered friends of God.

Christ also knew this holy fear. He obeyed until His mission was accomplished, even though it cost Him all!

Prayer

Father, You are holy. You are all powerful. I respect You, and I tremble in Your presence. You are both awesome and terrifying, and I revere Your name and Your ways. Most of all, I love You and serve You. Thank You for calling me Your own. Thank You for writing my name in Your Book of Life. Amen.

Day Thirty

What Are My Spiritual Gifts?

Just as we have many members in one body and
all the members do not have the same function, so we,
who are many, are one body in Christ,
and individually members one of another.
Since we have gifts that differ according to the grace given to us,
each of us is to exercise them accordingly.

—ROMANS 12:4–6

SOME OF US MAY FEEL SPIRITUALLY AWKWARD ABOUT FITTING INTO the body of Christ. We may feel as if we're the self-conscious hands attached to the extra-long arms, unsure what to do with ourselves. Maybe we're not sure what our role is, where we fit in, or what is expected of us. Maybe we wonder whether God even sees our awkward dilemma.

The answer is yes. He sees it. Even more, He wants you operating in and confident in your gift, because He has a specific spiritual purpose for your existence. You have a job God selected for you, one that only you can do. We all do. God has given each person certain abilities and a role to play using those gifts. And when we know what our spiritual gifts are, God can use us to do great things—even to change the world!

As you read the following list, do you see where you fit into the body? Have others sometimes commended you for anything on this list? Do you see gifts there you desire to have or gifts you're already exhibiting and using? Select one or two you think might be your gift.

- **Helps:** Through practical aid, you unselfishly meet others' needs.

- **Giving:** You give generously. You meet the needs of others.

- **Mercy:** You encourage those who are hurting and walk with them until they receive healing.

- **Encouragement:** You encourage others and remind them of God's powerful ways.

- **Wisdom:** You have godly insights that enable you to help guide others in their efforts to live a godly life.

- **Knowledge:** You memorize Scripture and help others use Scripture for decision making.

- **Discerning of spirits:** You're able to appraise the true motives of others, and you can sense whether something is from God or of either demonic or human origin.

- **Evangelism:** You carry a heavy burden for the lost and can effectively reach them.

- **Leadership:** You are people oriented and lead them into a deeper relationship with God and others.

- **Administration:** You can organize and implement plans. You lead others in ministry; you are goal oriented.

- **Teaching:** You can clearly communicate so that all who hear understand. You love to speak the truth.

- **Prophecy:** You receive divinely inspired messages and communicate them so others are convicted, encouraged, or challenged.

- **Hospitality:** You reach out and warmly welcome others into your home.

- **Pastor/Shepherd:** You are an overseer. You care for the well-being of the body. You protect, guide, and lead.

- **Apostleship:** You plant new ministries and churches. You are an influencer. A missionary.

- **Miracles:** You are extra sensitive to the moving of the Holy Spirit. You desire God to reveal Himself and to draw many to Him.

- **Healing:** You are compassionate for the sick. You want physical, emotional, or spiritual restoration.

When we use our gifts, we are building God's kingdom. And when we use our gifts to encourage others to exercise *their* spiritual gifts, we are working along with the Holy Spirit to fulfill God's perfect will on this earth. How cool is that?

Final Thoughts and Questions

I asked above which gifts you think God has given you. Have you used those gifts much? What ways can you see yourself nurturing these gifts? How can you use them today?

> **Prayer**
>
> *Father, I want to exercise the spiritual gifts You've given me. Help me to nurture my gifts, grow them to maturity, and use them for Your kingdom. Give me more opportunities to use them. Be glorified in my life and through my gifts. Amen.*

Day Thirty-One

God's Intricate Design for My Life

For thou didst form my inward parts:
Thou didst cover me in my mother's womb.
I will give thanks unto thee; for I am fearfully and wonderfully
*   made:*
Wonderful are thy works;
And that my soul knoweth right well.
My frame was not hidden from thee,
When I was made in secret,
And curiously wrought in the lowest parts of the earth.
Thine eyes did see mine unformed substance;
And in thy book they were all written,
Even the days that were ordained for me.

—PSALM 139:13–16 ASV

GOD KNEW YOU BEFORE YOU WERE FASHIONED IN YOUR MOTHER'S womb. He knew the number of hairs on your head, He memorized your fingerprints, He tweaked your personality and possibly your nose. He loved you then and He loves you now. You are not an accident! God planned your life and fashioned you for a reason. You are a perfect soul with a spark of the Father glowing and living within you. The Master Architect drew up detailed blueprints for you. What a profound picture of love. You have a purpose for living and breathing.

Maybe God created you to be a mom so you can pour Christ's love and wisdom into your children, or a scientist so you can discover great cures for diseases. Or maybe an artist who paints pictures that inspire others to think about God or a carpenter who builds homes for families. Whatever it is you were created to do, God has a reason, and that reason *always* involves helping others and thereby glorifying the Father.

The main purpose for which you were created is to serve others. God tells us the perfect religion is to take care of the widows and orphans (James 1:27). He also tells us He wants us to "loosen the bonds of wickedness, to undo the bands of the yoke, and to let the oppressed go free" (Isa. 58:6). To "break every yoke," to divide your bread with the hungry, to bring the homeless poor into the house, and to clothe the naked (vv. 6–7).

Did you know that in addition you were created to find Him and know Him? "They would seek God, if perhaps they might grope for Him and find Him" (Acts 17:27).

You were made to glorify Him: "All Your works shall give thanks to You, O Lord, and Your godly ones shall bless You" (Ps. 145:10).

You were fashioned to see His power: "For since the creation of the world His invisible attributes, His eternal power and divine nature, have been clearly seen, being understood through what has been made, so that they are without excuse" (Rom. 1:20).

You were created to see His glory and His handiwork: "The heavens are telling of the glory of God; and their expanse is declaring the work of His hands" (Ps. 19:1).

You were created to witness His wisdom: "O Lord, how many are Your works! In wisdom You have made them all; the earth is full of Your possessions" (Ps. 104:24).

Prayer

Father, I am Your servant. May Your purpose come alive in me. Help me to fulfill that purpose every day of my life for Your honor and glory! Amen.

Christlike Attitudes

Christ's teachings focus on helping us to change our core attitudes. He knew core attitudes shape core actions. This phase helps us to confront our unhealthy, self-centered attitudes and transform them into Christ-centered "Be-Attitudes" to help us "be" like Christ!

Day Thirty-Two

Blessed Are
the Poor in Spirit

"Blessed are the poor in spirit,
for theirs is the kingdom of heaven."
—MATTHEW 5:3 NIV

MANY PEOPLE BELIEVE THE TRUTHS IN THE SERMON ON THE MOUNT are the core of all Jesus's sermons. Everything Christ spoke on and preached about can be summed up in these truths. And because the Beatitudes in Matthew 5 are seemingly opposite of our natural inclinations, they cause us to look at life from a different angle—a God angle. They help us focus on God and others more than self. That's why Jesus taught the truths in the Beatitudes over and over again. That's why everything else He taught points back to these truths.

"Blessed are the poor in spirit, for theirs is the kingdom of heaven" (Matt. 5:3 NIV).

Blessed: Who is the woman who is poor in spirit, the woman who inherits the kingdom of heaven? The woman who has deep, untouchable joy, a secret joy that does not depend on circumstances. This woman has the blessings of God.

Are the poor in spirit: This woman is constantly aware of the "poor" spiritual state of her soul. She remembers the weight of her sins. She remembers how her sins have broken the Father's heart. She is not merely "poor in spirit" but is like a beggar who is totally destitute of pride.

"Two men went up to the temple to pray, one a Pharisee and the other a tax collector. The Pharisee stood by himself and prayed: 'God, I thank you that I am not like other people—robbers, evildoers, adulterers—or even like this tax collector' ... But the tax collector stood at a distance. He would not even look up to heaven, but beat his breast and said, 'God, have mercy on me, a sinner.'" (Luke 18:10–11, 13 NIV)

This tax collector is a perfect example of one who is poor in spirit. He knew there was no righteousness in him alone. He was spiritually broke! He clung to God's mercy and was totally emptied of self-pride, self-righteousness, and self-centeredness.

Our culture today is full of arrogant, narcissistic, puffed-up people who wreak havoc on their families, on society, and all who come in contact with them. Their haughty attitude creates chaos wherever they go and for whomever they are with. Can you imagine a society where everyone is living so selfishly? It would be beyond horrible! But what if we all decided to take Christ's advice and live as if we were poor in spirit? A society living with this attitude would be heavenly.

For theirs is the kingdom of heaven. This kingdom is both futuristic and present. It is really an upside-down kingdom—the poor, not the rich, get in.

Blessed with God's approval is the woman emptied of all self. She knows everything she is in life comes from God's hands. She purposely separates herself from sin so that she can be attached to and in good communion with God, with her eyes open to God's upside-down kingdom.

She remembers her sins so that she remembers not to return to them. She remembers how the shame of her sin caused a chasm between her and God. She does not carry the guilt of her sins, since Christ faithfully removed them (as far as the east is from the west). She is washed clean. But she remembers. She remembers how easy it was to fall into sin. She remembers how weak she is when depending on her own might. She remembers that she needs the help of the Holy Spirit to overcome. She remembers that she cannot judge others harshly, since she herself is a sinner saved by the grace of God.

When she remembers, she is following Christ's advice and being poor in spirit. Hers is the kingdom of heaven.

Final Thoughts and Questions

Do you remember how bad you felt the last time you caught yourself in a sin? Did you wonder if your sin broke Father's heart? This is what it means to be poor in spirit. Let's strive to remember this sorrow the next time we are tempted to sin.

Prayer

Blessed are You, oh Lord, Deliverer and King of my soul. Please change my selfish heart into a poor-in-spirit heart. Help me to experience and learn from the sorrow sin brings. Help me to live like Your holy Son today and every day. Have mercy on me. I am a sinner in need of You. I love you. Amen.

Day Thirty-Three

Blessed Are
Those Who Mourn

*"Blessed are those who mourn,
for they will be comforted."*
—MATTHEW 5:4 NIV

WHAT IS CHRIST CALLING US TO DO WHEN HE CALLS THOSE WHO mourn blessed? We think of mourning primarily as the expression of great sorrow for someone who has died. But what does mourning mean for us spiritually? Are we to help comfort the ones who mourn? Are we supposed to be in mourning ourselves?

Or is He saying that our own sin should cause us to mourn? That our sin should cause us deep, gut-wrenching sorrow, as if someone close to us had died? What if we were in anguish over our sins? What if our hearts were so tuned into God's heart that we were constantly, intensely aware of how our sins break His heart? What if we lose sleep and can barely concentrate on anything else because of our sin's all-consuming torment? Is this what Christ meant by mourning?

Yes, I think it is. But I think there is more.

Mourning is also the ability to feel the hurts of others, especially those who are sinned against. Therefore, we are blessed with God's approval when we care for and are compassionate about the sufferings of others. When we help the victims of abuse, of sexual assault, and of injustice as well as the hurting, broken, and bruised reeds of this world, we are blessed with a grieving spirit. Blessed, because we don't rebel against the pain, nor do we avoid it. Instead we let what breaks God's heart break our own.

118

Blessed with God's approval and profound joy is the woman who allows heartache to motivate her to go out and make a difference, to right the wrongs. She chooses to go through the pain because she knows out of true pain comes true repentance.

Blessed with God's approval is the woman who mourns over her neighbor's sins, over her nation's sins, and over the violence and greed in this world. Blessed with God's approval is the woman who visits the sick, helps the needy, and listens to the problems of those around her. She visits the infirm, the prisoners, and the elderly.

Final Thoughts and Questions

My challenge to you, dear reader, is to seek and find the hurting in your neighborhood. Listen to their hearts. Visit them in hospitals. Help them through their grief. Help them turn their mourning into joy.

Prayer

Father, break my heart for what breaks Yours. Give me strength and wisdom to help the hurting. Lead me to them. Give me healing words to say and ideas for how to help. Amen.

Day Thirty-Four

Blessed Are the Meek

"Blessed are the meek,
for they will inherit the earth."
—MATTHEW 5:5 NIV

MEEKNESS IS NOT WEAKNESS. MEEKNESS IMPLIES SOMETHING POW-erful brought under complete control, such as a powerful horse brought under control by the little bit in its mouth. I think that's the kind of meekness Jesus advises us to emulate. And what is more pow-erful, what has greater need of being brought under complete control, than our own emotions?

Controlling our emotions is one of the hardest challenges we face. We are emotionally driven people. From time to time, we can even find ourselves justifying our out-of-control emotions by saying, "This is just how God made me." In addition, God seems to have made our gender, as a whole, more sensitive compared to men, and learning to control our emotions can be difficult.

But as disciples, we must overcome. When we control our emo-tions instead of letting them control us, we're making serious headway on our spiritual remodeling project.

Jesus is the greatest example of this kind of emotional meekness. He never acted in revenge or anger. He was not a hothead or cruel. He always had perfect control of all His emotions. That is not to say unrighteousness did not arouse powerful feelings in Him. After all,

He drove out those who defiled His Father's temple. He was full of zeal, but He was in control.

I think the finest example of Jesus's incredible might brought under God's control was when He was in the garden of Gethsemane the night of His arrest. He could have uttered a single command to bring a myriad of angels to defend Him. But instead He submitted to God's will and offered Himself as the sacrifice for humanity's sin. This is the kind of meekness for which we should all strive.

Another aspect of meekness is humbleness. Not a doormat kind of humble, but the humility a woman exhibits when she knows she is a child of the King, yet is humble enough to serve people. Her meekness is an outward expression of inner strength and spiritual refinement.

In his book *The Pursuit of God*, A. W. Tozer said, "The meek man is not a human mouse afflicted with a sense of his own inferiority. Rather, he may be in his moral life as bold as a lion and as strong as Samson, but he has stopped being fooled about himself. He has accepted God's estimate of his own life. He knows he is as weak and helpless as God declares him to be, but paradoxically, he knows at the same time that he is in the sight of God of more importance than angels. In himself—nothing. In God—everything, that is his motto" (Wilder, 2008, p. 55).

Blessed with God's approval is the woman who works hard at controlling her emotions. Blessed is the woman who is meek enough to serve her Father's subjects. Blessed is the woman who knows she is nothing, but in God she is everything! This woman inherits the earth.

Final Thoughts and Questions

Choose one emotion you have a hard time controlling. Ask for the Holy Spirit to help you control it, and work hard at catching and controlling that emotion today.

Prayer

Blessed are You, oh God, my King, who blesses those who have brought their emotions under Your perfect control. You bless those whose emotions line up with Your commands. You bless those who realize they are nothing in themselves but are everything in You. Help me to be meek like this. Amen.

Blessed Are Those Who Hunger after Righteousness

*"Blessed are those who hunger
and thirst for righteousness,
for they will be filled."*
—MATTHEW 5:6 NIV

IN THIS BEATITUDE, I BELIEVE, CHRIST IS TELLING US TO GO AFTER righteousness like a hungry or thirsty person would go after a morsel of food or a cup of cool water. I believe we all have at our core a strong yearning or void that must be filled with something other than and greater than ourselves. But not everyone fills that ache with God. Some people fill it with material possessions, accomplishments, or even chocolate—all of which will turn to rubble or fat. God wants us to fill that void with righteousness. And righteousness does not disappear or turn into jiggly goo—it is eternal.

What is righteousness? The Hebrew word means "just, innocent, and one who is in the right" (www.Biblehub.com). The Bible tells us what righteousness is and how we can achieve it:

- God directs us to righteousness. "He restores my soul; He guides me in the paths of righteousness for His name's sake" (Ps. 23:3).

- Righteousness is an attribute of God. "My tongue shall declare Your righteousness" (Ps. 35:28).

- Righteousness and the Law (the first five books of the Bible) go hand in hand. "Let my tongue sing of thy word; for all thy commandments [laws] are righteousness" (Ps. 119:172 ASV).

- Righteousness is the exact opposite of wickedness. "Thou hast loved righteousness, and hated wickedness" (Ps. 45:7 ASV).

- Righteousness keeps us on the way to God. "Righteousness guards the one whose way is blameless, but wickedness subverts the sinner" (Prov. 13:6).

- Righteousness will be the standard by which we are judged on judgment day—when the books are opened (John 16:8 and Acts 17:31).

The Bible says our actions and words prove our righteousness—or lack thereof. Noah was righteous despite his surroundings. And remember, his surroundings were so vile that God destroyed every human outside the ark, meaning that Noah's surroundings were much worse than ours.

When we hunger for this kind of righteousness—ethically right, truthful, and obedient to the commandments of God—our spiritual bellies will be filled. When we thirst after the kind of righteousness that brings physical and spiritual healing—the righteousness that is the standard by which we will all be judged—our spiritual thirst will be quenched! God will see to it.

Jesus lived the most righteous life. He never sinned and He always obeyed His Father. His life oozed righteous acts. When we surrender our lives to Jesus as our Messiah, His blood covers our sin and makes us righteous. It is only through *Him* that we are forgiven and clean. But when we model our lives after Christ's life, we too can have lives that ooze righteous acts.

Final Thoughts and Questions

How much do you want righteousness? How intense is your desire? Would you charge after it like a starving man would for a morsel of food? Do you ever settle for partial righteousness? Or do you long for complete right standing before God?

Prayer

Father, help me to walk righteously before You. Shine a spotlight on areas that need to be remodeled. Send the Holy Spirit to give me the strength to make changes. Help me to look like You in every single area of my life so I can please You, my good Father. I love You! Amen.

Blessed Are
the Merciful

"Blessed are the merciful,
for they will be shown mercy."
—MATTHEW 5:7 NIV

TODAY'S VERSE SEEMS STRAIGHTFORWARD. IF YOU WANT MERCY, then you need to show mercy. *Mercy* means "showing compassion, forbearance, pity, sympathy, forgiveness, kindness, tenderness, or refraining from harming offenders" (from *The Gospel of Matthew* by David Barclay in The Daily Bible Study Series, Westminster Press, 1975, p. 103). The Hebrew word *chesedh* is an untranslatable word that means not only are we to sympathize with another, but we are to get into their skin. We are to see what they see, feel what they feel, and think what they think. We are to make their pain our pain. Thus, mercy is much more than a fleeting emotion of pity. It's a deliberate act of identifying another's pain and making it our own.

In God's kingdom we must give to receive, be last to be first, lose to find, serve to rule, strive to be least—not greatest—and be merciful to get mercy. This kind of kingdom thinking doesn't come naturally; it takes a mind overhaul.

Part of that overhaul is learning that God has forgiven our many sins so we might forgive and be merciful to others. Father God is our ultimate model of mercy. He never shielded Himself from the world's pain. In fact, He sent His only Son to literally get into our flesh, into our minds, and into our world. Jesus took on the flesh of mankind and faced every type of temptation and trial we have faced. "He had to be made like his brethren in all things, so that He might become a merciful and faithful high priest in things pertaining to God" (Heb. 2:17).

God's nature is to show mercy. His disciplines are always perfectly balanced between impartial justice and unmerited mercy. Yet in His great love for us He deals out chastisements, because without chastisement we would be likely to continue making the same mistakes over and over. Even His disciplines are rooted in mercy. They are for our own good.

Final Thoughts and Questions

- Has mercy ever been shown to you? When?

- Are you quick to judge and confront, or are you quick to offer sweet mercy?

Prayer

Blessed are You, oh God, our King. You bless those who realize their own spiritual bankruptcy and those who mourn deeply over their own sin. You bless those who strive to make their emotions line up with Your Word, and you bless those who desire more than anything to walk righteously before You. Oh God, You bless those who can get into others' minds to see what they see, think what they think, and feel what they feel. Help me to live out these attitudes. Amen.

Day Thirty-Seven

Blessed Are
the Pure in Heart

"Blessed are the pure in heart,
for they will see God."
—MATTHEW 5:8 NIV

IN A SENSE, OUR BODIES ARE LIKE SPIRITUAL TEMPLES, AND OUR hearts are like the holy of holies—the place where the Spirit of God dwells. The heart is what defines us, where our emotions, our affections, and our perceptions live. God is concerned about our hearts. "Man looks at the outward appearance, but the LORD looks at the heart" (1 Sam. 16:7).

To be "pure in heart" should be every disciple's goal. In fact, all the previous Beatitudes must be mastered first to achieve a pure heart. We must recognize our own spiritual depravity and be *poor in spirit,* we must *mourn* over our own poor spiritual state, *meekly* submit our emotions to God's control, and *hunger and thirst* after righteousness to purify our hearts.

Some people's minds are filthy. They can twist any situation, no matter how innocent or beautiful, into a crude joke. Because their hearts are dirty, everything they see is dirty. Their irrepressible vulgarities turn everything they are involved with into something unclean. For some, their every ambition is for self-gain. Others have hearts hard and unrepentant. Some have hearts full of anger, greed, lies, and selfishness. Others justify their sin. Their hearts are not pure. God is calling us away from this type of low living, because with God, it is all about the heart. He wants it clean and pure.

When our hearts are pure, we can look at each other with the eyes of Christ. We no longer see each other as potential annoyances or opponents, but as the beautiful children of God we all are. We can see God in each other. This is what I believe Jesus wants us to strive for.

Blessed with the great approval of God and deep untouchable joy is the woman who works hard at keeping her heart clean before God. This woman will see God.

Final Thoughts and Questions

We women can be judgmental toward one another. We judge intellect, fashion (or lack of), speech, hair, attitude, and so on. We do it without even thinking about it, as if it were second nature. These judgments do not flow from a pure heart. Is this an area where you (like most women!) need to clean up your heart?

Other areas of our hearts that may need some remodeling are gossiping, coveting, envying, flirting, grumbling, comparing, and manipulating. Whatever the issue, let's purify it.

Prayer

Blessed are You, oh God, our King, who blesses those whose hearts are pure. You bless them by allowing them to see Your beautiful being. Help me to have clean hands and a pure heart. Amen.

Blessed Are the Peacemakers

"Blessed are the peacemakers,
for they will be called children of God."
—MATTHEW 5:9 NIV

WORLD PEACE IS AN IDEA THAT ORIGINATED IN HEAVEN. IT IS A beautiful longing of every human heart. God hardwired us in such a way that peace is important to us. It is also important to our fellow neighbors, to the world, and to God. But we can't have peace unless we have individuals who love it and are willing to negotiate for it. A peacemaker is such a person. She seeks to bring unity and understanding between those who are divided.

The Hebrew word for peace is *shalom*, which means not only the absence of strife but also the presence of everything good. To say *shalom* to someone pronounces this blessing on them: *I hope for you not only the absence of all harm but also the presence of everything that is good.*

I really dislike confrontations. I confess that I'm often guilty of saying whatever needs to be said to dodge them. And when I do, I sometimes give myself credit for being a peacemaker. My sister helped me to see how fake this is. "Mary," she said, "that kind of 'peace' is perverted. It's not real. It's not the truth." She was right, as usual, but I must admit I still struggle. Sometimes it's hard for me to "disturb the peace," even if that peace is fake. In this area, I am a work in progress, and I'm writing this for my own growth. I'm learning how to be a true peacemaker.

A true peacemaker builds bridges through the often-painful process of addressing problems in an attempt to resolve them in a way that results in greater harmony. And yes, sometimes that can be confrontational. A true peacemaker sows seeds of peace by digging with tenderness to find out what is causing hostility between the parties—even if one of the parties is herself.

Peacemakers are also evangelists, because they help restore the lost back to the Prince of Peace. This beatitude calls peacemakers "children of God" for a reason: they are like their Father, the true peacemaker, in that for every way they stray away from Him, He gives them a million ways to return.

Jesus is the ultimate peacemaker. He made peace between a holy God and a sinful, unclean humanity. He reconciled us with God. In fact, the whole Bible is about this perfect act of peacemaking. How beautiful!

Final Thoughts and Questions

Are you a true peacemaker? Do you confront just to make your point, or do you confront to search for truth and bring peace? Do you avoid confrontation and, like me, say whatever you need to say to dodge the bullet? What are some ways you can become a true peacemaker today? At work? At home? In your family?

Prayer

Blessed are You, oh God, my King, who blesses those who imitate Your heavenly trait of peacemaking. Help me to love peace as You do, and help me to be like Jesus, a true peacemaker in every sense of that word. Amen.

Blessed Are
Those Persecuted
for Christ's Sake

*Blessed are those who are persecuted because of righteousness,
for theirs is the kingdom of heaven. Blessed are you
when people insult you, persecute you and falsely say all kinds
of evil against you because of me. Rejoice and be glad,
because great is your reward in heaven, for in the same way
they persecuted the prophets who were before you.*
—MATTHEW 5:10–12 NIV

IT'S HARD FOR ME TO IMAGINE EXTREME, LIFE-THREATENING PERSE-cution because I live comfortably here in Texas. But I know many of my brothers and sisters in Christ are facing harsh persecution all over the world. In China, forty million Christians must worship in underground churches to avoid persecution. In Muslim nations, when a convert to Christ is uncovered, she must denounce Jesus, become a slave, or opt for death. ISIS is beheading Christians. According to information recently released by the Pew Research Center, 75 percent of the world's population lives in areas with severe religious restrictions (www.opendoorsusa.org). And, according to the U.S. Department of State, Christians in more than sixty countries face persecution from their own government or from people nearby simply for believing in Jesus Christ.

The early church faced severe punishments for following Jesus as well. Some were thrown to the lions, and others faced slow, painful deaths through a variety of cruel methods. Some were soaked in pitch and lit as torches for the Roman ruler's gardens, some were crucified, and others were disemboweled on the executioner's table. Sadly, history is chock-full of persecutions such as these. Jesus, who foresaw the future, was warning His disciples. He is warning us too. Be prepared and be ready for persecution. It is coming.

Maybe we won't face extreme persecution for righteousness' sake. Maybe it will be slightly less painful—snubs and slanders, our words being twisted, insults, sneers, and other forms of cruelty. Even though that type of persecution is less severe, it still is difficult to face. Whether extreme or mild, persecution because of our Christian faith will happen to all of us. Why? Because much of the world hates Christ and therefore hates His followers.

Jesus tells us to rejoice when persecution happens. Here again, we have a picture of God's upside-down kingdom. When people are cruel to us, God wants us to rejoice rather than become angry and eager for revenge. I must be honest: rejoicing over snubs is not my first nature—or even my second or third. Being a disciple is tough! It is some of the hardest, most humbling work *ever*! But Jesus told us to rejoice for a reason: once we've mastered the joy response, He gives us something incredible to look forward to, something that will leave our minds reeling in delirious excitement.

We are to rejoice in the face of persecution because the kingdom of heaven is ours. *Ours!* A kingdom where there will be no more tears or sorrow. No more pain or suffering. No more sickness or death. No more insults or snubs. A kingdom filled with every good thing. A kingdom that never ends. Just think about that. Let it sink in. This indeed is a great reward.

Final Thoughts and Questions

Are you being persecuted because of your faith? How can you embrace that persecution today? How can you turn it into a blessing?

Prayer

Father, help me rejoice in persecution. Help me catch a glimpse of Your kingdom and then let it settle in my spirit forevermore. Help me to stay focused on Your kingdom more than I focus on this earthly kingdom. I love You, Father. Amen.

PHASE
FIVE

Be Transformed, Not Conformed

Being transformed to the image of God's Son is a spiritually challenging process that takes energy, gumption, and the help of the Holy Spirit—as well as time. Much time. Many just give up. They lose sight of the goal of becoming like Jesus. They quit before they cross the finish line.

This phase cheers you on and encourages you to keep running the race. Don't quit!

Day Forty

Evidence of the Remodel

The fruit of the Spirit is love, joy, peace, patience,
kindness, goodness, faithfulness, gentleness, self-control;
against such things there is no law.
—GALATIANS 5:22–23

THE BIBLE TELLS US WE ARE NOT TO JUDGE EACH OTHER. JESUS even said, "Do not judge, or you too will be judged" (Matt. 7:1 NIV). We are told to instead observe and identify the spiritual "fruit" a person displays in his or her life. And not just in the lives of others; we should examine the fruit in our own lives as well.

This fruit of the Spirit is a major goal of spiritual remodeling. As we grow in spiritual maturity, our lives begin to abound in spiritual fruit. The fruit of the Spirit can't be counterfeited or hidden; it is either evident in a person's life or not there. It is not about busily doing "Christian-y" stuff, but about actively and passionately living out Jesus's words and becoming transformed into His image.

I always thought I was doing pretty well with this whole "fruit" thing, but then I ran across a "fruit assessment" test from a sermon John Ortberg preached to his congregation (see John Ortberg's "The Fruit of the Spirit" series, www.preachingtodayssermons.com). I took the test and was immediately humbled. I couldn't believe I had scored *soooo* low!

Hopefully you will score higher than I did. Take the test and see. For each fruit listed below, read the description and then rate yourself from one to ten—one identifying an area that needs vast improvement and ten identifying an area where you're already experiencing great success. If you score a perfect ten for each fruit, it's time for you to pack your bags. A fiery chariot will be by to pick you up and take you directly to heaven. You are righteous—as righteous as Elijah. First-class flight for you!

Here is the fruit—and the questions:

- **Love:** How tender is your heart toward God? Do you find yourself often serving others? Do you have a critical spirit in your heart?

- **Joy:** Is your irritability factor high or low? Do you speak words of complaint or encouragement? Do you laugh often? Do you choose joy instead of frustration?

- **Patience:** How do you respond when you don't get your way? Do you wait graciously? How do you handle it when people are slow?

- **Peace:** Are you at rest with God? Are you often troubled or worried? Would people describe you as content or discontent?

- **Gentle:** Do you often speak the truth in love? When you're angry, do you try to inflict pain to get even? Do you often give comfort to the hurting?

- **Kindness:** Do you lend a hand? Do you acknowledge people and notice them?

- **Generosity:** Do you give of yourself for public notice? Do you give the smallest amount possible?

- **Faithfulness:** Are you dependable? Do you ever use words to deceive? Do you procrastinate?

- **Self-Control:** Do you have any bad habits? Do you give in to impulses? How is your mouth control?

I warned you it would be painful.

Let God be our fruit inspector. Let God help us make changes in our fruitiness.

Final Thoughts and Questions

In what areas did you score low? As you go through today, try to be conscious of those areas. Work on transforming them from your current low score closer to a perfect ten.

Prayer

Father, help me bear good fruit. Help me become aware of the bad fruit in my life and transform it into good, holy fruit. Amen.

Day Forty-One

Fulfilling the Father's Will

*"For whoever does the will of My Father
who is in heaven, he is My brother and sister and mother."*
—MATTHEW 12:50

WE ARE SUCH NEEDY PEOPLE. WE NEED HOUSING, FOOD, WATER, clothes—not to mention pretty shoes and chocolate deliciousness. More important than these life-sustaining needs is our need for love. It's our most basic core need. Without it we cease to thrive.

When my youngest daughter was born severely premature, I went to the ICU every day to hold her and love on her. The doctors told me this act of nurturing did more for her than all their medicines and care. Because many of the babies in the ICU weren't held enough, the hospital brought in baby holders. Every day the only job these compassionate people had was to hold and kiss the babies. Love helped these little ones fight for life. Love helped them grow.

What is love? An emotion? A strong belief? An inner fire? Nope. Simply put, love is the act of meeting the needs of others, just as the baby holders meet the needs of many tiny babies by giving their time to snuggle, kiss, and nurture.

We know we humans have needs. But have you ever thought of God as having needs? Or more accurately stated, desires and wishes? It's a difficult concept to grasp, isn't it? After all, God is all-powerful. Everything comes from Him and resides in Him. How can He need anything other than what He already is? Yet in Matthew 7:21, Jesus tells us we must do the will of His Father. And guess what the definition of *will* is? Desires or wishes.

Yes, God our Father has desires and wishes He wants us to meet. Our meeting them or, for that matter, neglecting them does not change His love for us. Our heavenly Father's love is constant and unchanging. Our actions do, however, alter the condition of God's happiness. He can be overjoyed by our actions or He can be heartbroken by them, depending on what it is we have done.

Here's a short list of some of God's desires and wishes that, when we meet them, bring Him great joy:

- Love Him—Luke 10:27
- Fear Him—Matt. 10:28
- Love each other—Mark 12:31
- Hear His voice and hold fast to Him—John 10:27
- Obey Him—1 Sam. 15:22
- Keep His commandments by being covenant children—Ex. 19:5 and 2 John 1:6
- Serve Him with our whole being—Mark 12:33
- Praise Him—Ps. 150:3–6
- Worship Him in Bible study—Josh. 1:8 and Ps. 119:11

Our heavenly Father is our spiritual remodeling boss. All good bosses recognize hard workers and give rewards. They recognize wise workers and give raises. Our Father—our Big Boss—recognizes and appreciates our attempts to fulfill His will, and He generously rewards as well. His rewards go way beyond raises and other perks. His rewards are not only earthly-type blessings but eternal heavenly blessings. They never expire or lose their glitter. They are forever! Safely kept in a vault in God's kingdom, they wait for you to claim them.

I don't know about you, but the thought that my actions affect Father's heart is sobering. The more I get to know Him, the more I love Him, because with each passing year I discover more and more of what He has done for me. And the more I see what He's done for me, the more I want to please Him. And I please Him when I act like Jesus. I please Him when I meet His wishes and desires.

Final Thoughts and Questions

Can you name five other desires you think Father might have concerning you? As you go through this day, stop and ask yourself how you can fulfill those desires of His.

What kind of rewards do you think He is putting in your heavenly vault? Start wondering and dreaming big!

Prayer

Father, You are good and holy in all Your ways. Speak to me today. Open my eyes to how I can fulfill Your heart's desires. I want to please You. I want to make You proud. I want to build Your kingdom in my life. Amen.

Meeting the Needs
of Others

The whole Law is fulfilled in one word, in the statement,
"You shall love your neighbor as yourself."
—GALATIANS 5:14

OUR NEIGHBORS ARE THE PEOPLE WE DO LIFE WITH—OUR PARENTS, our kids, and the men we married. They are our coworkers, friends, and literal neighbors, the people who live near us. They are people in this spiritual remodeling process alongside us, fellow believers. All these neighbors are the people we are commanded to love as we love ourselves.

Since meeting the needs of others is the true way of showing unconditional love, we need to get to know our neighbors on a deeper level. We need to know how they think, how they act, and how they best receive love. In his book *The 5 Love Languages: The Secret to Love That Lasts,* Dr. Gary Chapman categorizes people's greatest love needs and how they best receive love from others. For some, receiving thoughtful gifts is the best way to receive love. For others, receiving encouraging and uplifting words is the best. Some people desire acts of service from others or long, soul-touching conversations. For still others, the desire for quality time together is their main love language. God made us all different, and it's important to study and understand our neighbors so we can show them love the way *they* need to be loved.

It's also important to understand how we best receive love because sometimes we tend to show our love to others the way we want to receive love. The results of that approach are often less than stellar, and that can leave us frustrated by the receiver's lack of joy or appreciation. By understanding ourselves better, we can better serve others. We can show them true love the way they need to receive it from us.

When we selflessly meet the needs of others in this way, we can make authentic connections with them that have the potential to be life-changing and even world changing. And the best thing about showing love in this way is that we are fulfilling one of Christ's greatest commissions: "As I have loved you, so you must love one another" (John 13:34 NIV).

Love is such an amazing gift! Love truly is the meaning of life.

Final Thoughts and Questions

Make a list of those neighbors closest to you. Start experimenting with showing love in different ways. Give a gift—watch their response. Have a heart-to-heart talk—note their response. Serve them, speak encouraging words to them, or them give a warm hug. What is their response?

It also helps to watch how your neighbors show love to others. That may well be how they like to receive love.

Prayer

Father, I want to build Your kingdom on this earth. Give me wisdom as I endeavor to meet my neighbors' needs. Give me insight into my husband's love needs, my family's love needs, my parents' love needs, and my siblings' love needs. Give me a selfless attitude so I can fulfill their needs and build stronger connections, thereby pointing them to Your Son. Amen.

Day Forty-Three

I Can't Do This
by Myself

For this cause we also, since the day we heard it,
do not cease to pray for you, and to desire
that ye might be filled with the knowledge of his will
in all wisdom and spiritual understanding.
—COLOSSIANS 1:9 KJV

HERE'S THE SET-UP:

At one particularly difficult job site I found myself on scaffolding twenty-five-feet high, trying to hold a board in place so my husband could super-stretch from the roof joist, where he was precariously perched, and nail-gun the board securely in place. The problem was I couldn't quite hold the board in the proper position while I was still *inside* the scaffolding frame.

Now, here's what happened:

I look down from the top platform of the bright-yellow scaffolding. "So high," I mutter as I climb outside of the frame and wrap my left hand around the rail to hold on. With my other hand I swing the board up and hold it in place so Tony can nail-gun it securely. One nail is all we need. One nail and I can climb back into the safety of the scaffolding frame. "We've got this," I say with as much bravado as I can muster.

I speak too soon. Tony lines up the board, presses the trigger, and the nail gun fires, bounces, and then double fires. Not usually a problem, except today. The second bounce accidentally nail-guns my glove to the roof joist—while my hand is still in it. Thankfully it misses my flesh and bones and nails only the glove. But with one hand nailed to the roof and the other death-gripping the scaffolding, I'm in quite a pickle. To make it worse, my grip on the scaffolding is growing weak.

"Tony, I need help," I gasp.

Judging from the urgency in his voice, the look on my face must have spoken volumes. "Did I get your finger?" he asks, eyes bugging.

I shake my head. "Just my glove. But I can't get my hand out of it and my other grip is starting to slip." I fight panic.

Tony quickly, like the monkey he is, s-t-r-e-t-c-h-e-s a little closer and pries the nail out of my glove. I swing back to the scaffolding, grab on with my now-freed hand, and climb back inside to safety. We look at each other and nervously giggle. "That was a close one," I say.

If my coworker/husband hadn't been there to help me, I might still be hanging there to this day. I desperately needed the help of my coworker.

We all need others involved in our lives. We need someone who prays for us, holds us accountable in our walk before the Father, and helps us when we're in a pickle. An accountability partner does all these things.

Merriam-Webster's Collegiate Dictionary says *accountability* is a "willingness to accept responsibility . . . for one's actions." An accountability partner is someone willing to accept responsibility for holding us accountable for our choices and actions. They partner with us in our spiritual remodeling process.

David and Jonathan are prime examples of this kind of relationship. These two men, who really should have hated each other's guts, became a spiritual dynamic duo. One was the son of the king and the other was the son of a farmer. The one with birthrights to the throne willingly gave them to the lowly shepherd who had God rights to the throne. Together, they battled the enemy (by praying for each other), protected each other from the hand of death (in this case, Jonathan's own father), had close fellowship (listened to each other's hearts), and kept each other in balance (taught spiritual lessons to each other). Theirs was a bond that lasted until death. Theirs was a bond that made history.

Do you have an accountability partner? Do you have someone who knows your heart, your struggles, and your victories? Do you have someone who prays for you, admonishes you if needed, and encourages you in your spiritual walk? If you don't, now would be a great time to start searching her out.

We women need each other. We are hardwired to need female connections. We are hardwired to need an accountability partner/friend. I had gone too many years without one. For too many years, I felt that yearning for a deep friendship—but never took the steps to make it happen. Recently, I asked my sister to be my accountability partner, and it has been such a blessing. She knows me. She tells me the truth in love. She prays for me. She encourages me when I need it. She is invaluable to me. This was one of the best choices I've ever made.

She has many qualities I want and need in an accountability friend. I need someone strong enough to be hard on me when I need it. I need someone kind, someone growing spiritually, and someone who thinks a little differently than I do to help me see from a different perspective. I need someone who knows me well, someone I feel completely comfortable with, and someone I trust completely. My sister is all these things.

Final Thoughts and Questions

Do you have an accountability friend? If not, list the qualities you're looking for. List the areas where you desperately need an accountability partner's help (relationships, habits). (Also list the spiritual strengths you can offer to someone else.)

Now list the people you know who possess the qualities you've just listed, and then go to that person and explain what kind of relationship you'd like to have with them. Ask if they would be willing to pray for you and to accept your prayers in return. Invite their encouragement and their holding you accountable. Make sure to reciprocate.

Prayer

Father, lead me to that sister who will grow with me through life. Bring her face to my mind. Give me the words to say as I invite her on a spiritual journey together. Thank You, Lord. Amen.

Don't Resist Advice

Give instruction to a wise man and he will be still wiser,
teach a righteous man and he will increase his learning.
—PROVERBS 9:9

Listen to counsel and accept discipline,
that you may be wise.
—PROVERBS 19:20

I LIKE TO FIGURE THINGS OUT ON MY OWN—UNLESS, OF COURSE, it's a technical issue. Anything related to programming the TV or downloading computer stuff I am more than willing to hand off to someone else. But if it's anything hands-on, I just want to get in there, tear it apart, and figure it out all by myself.

I once took my vacuum cleaner apart to try to figure out and fix its many problems. As I was digging into its guts, my husband said, "You should write down all these steps in order. Or at least draw a diagram, so you can put it back together correctly." I tuned him out with a mumble. The steps seemed simple. I was sure I could remember them; I'm not a dummy. But, of course, when I went to put it all back together, I had lots of leftover parts scattered across my kitchen floor. Because I hadn't been willing to take the advice of someone wiser about electronic maintenance, I had to spend some hard-earned cash and humbly buy a brand-new vacuum. My heart had been stubborn— just the opposite of teachable.

It's important to our Father that we have teachable hearts. As a parent, I get frustrated when my children think they know how to do a job better than I do. Our Father is no different. He loves it when we say, "Teach me how, Father," instead of, "I can do this without You."

Why do we always think we can figure out life on our own? When we try, we muddle it up and have pieces left over. We need the help of God and of each other. That's how we're hardwired.

To many of us, it's often so hard—but so wise—to listen to the counsel of someone who wants to help and who is qualified to do so, like my husband with that stupid vacuum cleaner. Asking for advice doesn't make us look foolish. Asking for advice from someone more wise and knowledgeable makes us look wise. In fact, the Bible tells us to let the older instruct the younger. Smart advice!

It all comes down to results. What are the benefits of seeking wise advice and of having a teachable heart willing to follow that advice? It can save us from financial headache, relationship heartache, and spiritual soul ache, just to name a few. When we go to our wiser elders, brothers, or sisters and ask for their godly advice, their counsel may spare us from a terrible outcome. The benefits are great indeed—physically, emotionally, and spiritually.

Final Thoughts and Questions

Do you have any areas in your life where you resist instruction and advice? Has anyone come to you and pointed out unhealthy areas in your life? Do you need to repent of having a stubborn, unteachable heart? Then please, repent. Set your pride aside and listen to wise, godly counsel. It will go well with you when you do.

Prayer

Father, I need You! Help my heart to always stay teachable and soft toward You. Thank You for bringing people into my life who can give me wise counsel. I love You! Amen.

Day Forty-Five

Show Gratitude for Timely Help

Whatever you do in word or deed, do all in the name of the Lord Jesus, giving thanks through him to God the Father.
—COLOSSIANS 3:17

HAVE YOU EVER BENT OVER BACKWARD TO HELP SOMEONE, AFTER which they didn't give you a single word of thanks? How did that make you feel? When that happens to me, my response is, *I'm never helping that person again as long as I live!* Maybe I'm exaggerating a little, but not by much.

Talking about this reminds me of all the times I've mistreated God in the same way. I daily ask Him for things: protecting my family, providing income, helping a lost brother or sister or child come back to the fold. These requests are important, and regularly God answers them. But instead of telling Him thanks, I go on my merry way. Then the next day I send in my request list again, expecting God to answer those requests as well. I bet He gets kind of tired of my ungrateful attitude. If the roles were reversed, I know I would start feeling as though I was being taken advantage of.

As disciples of Jesus, we have so much to be thankful for. Because of Him we have victory over death and the grave (1 Cor. 15:54) and we have been given wisdom from on high (Dan. 2:23). We can be thankful for our faith (Rom. 1:8), for love (2 Thess. 1:3), for God's presence (Ps. 75:1), for ministries (1 Tim. 1:12), and for how our daily needs are met (Rom. 14:6). Colossians 3:17 reminds us, "Whatever you do, whether in word or deed, do it all in the name of the Lord Jesus, giving thanks to God the Father through him" (NIV).

If I could just learn to say thank you for *all* the ways our Father has taken care of me. If before my eyes slam shut at the end of every day I could get into the habit of talking to my Daddy Most High, saying, "Thank You for all You have done for me, and for all You have given me this day. I praise Your holy name." Those words would bless His heart; they would minister to Him. It blesses *my* heart to know that my thank-yous bless *His* heart.

Final Thoughts and Questions

Make a list of everything Father has blessed you with today, then tell Him thanks!

Prayer

Oh Most High God, thank You for all Your provisions and all Your blessings this day. Thank You for shelter, clothes, and food. Thank You for family, friends, and love. Thank You for Your holy, beautiful Son. Thank You for redemption. Thank You for Your great love. I love You, Father. I praise your holy name! Amen.

Contaminated Ground? Get Rid of It!

> *Peter came to Jesus and asked, "Lord, how many times*
> *shall I forgive my brother or sister who sins against me?*
> *Up to seven times?" Jesus answered, "I tell you,*
> *not seven times, but seventy-seven times."*
> —MATTHEW 18:21–22 NIV

ALL OF US WHO LIVE AND BREATHE GO THROUGH EXPERIENCES that make an impact and shape our heart and emotions and way of thinking. Some experiences are good and healthy; others are harmful and deadly. Some of these experiences are so toxic that they not only harm how we think but also place everyone around us at risk. When our past experiences cause us to treat others poorly—even people who had nothing to do with those experiences—our ground has become contaminated.

Contaminants come in many types. Some contamination we allow into our lives, such as addictions, devaluing God's Word and Christ, and sexual promiscuity in all its forms. Other contaminants have been dumped upon us—we have been sinned against. I'm speaking of poisons such as physical abuse, verbal and psychological abuse, neglect, rejection, abandonment, family dysfunction, and the lack of parental connection. In this daily reading, let's look at this second type of toxins, deadly poisons we need to excavate out of our lives.

Christ, in His great love for us, wants them completely gone. He knows if we're not able to deal with them in a healthy fashion, they will stunt spiritual growth, cause emotional and psychological sicknesses, and prevent our hearts from responding to Him. Worse yet, they keep our ears from hearing the truth of the Word. Sometimes these contaminants influence our minds to concentrate on *justification*—meaning that we *blame* our past instead of *cleaning up* our past.

A contractor cannot build on contaminated ground. He must clean it up before he can build on it. Christ too wants us to clean up our ground before we build. He knows contaminants rise to the surface and cause all manner of harm. Because He loves us so much, He wants us to dig out the contaminants resulting from sins committed against us and send them back to hell, where they came from. He wants the ground of our lives to be pure, clean, righteous, and holy. But how do we go about cleaning our ground? Do we need a shovel? Or do we need a bulldozer?

Start by honestly assessing the amount of contamination that has been dumped into your heart and asking yourself how it got there. (Were you abused or abandoned?) Who contaminated your ground? (Name them.) What does your contamination look like? (What are your symptoms?) What physical, mental, or spiritual scars has it left in your life? How is it hindering your relationships with others? How is it hindering your relationship with God? How is it keeping you in an unhealthy state? Write all these things down.

The best way to clean up your contaminated ground is Christ's way—it's all about forgiveness. He showed us how to forgive those who have harmed us in the past, and He shows us how to forgive those who are harming us right now: by deliberately praying for their good—spiritual good, physical good, and emotional good.

This is how we clean our contaminated soil. Some of you may need only a shovel. You purpose to forgive, even if you must forgive a thousand times a day, and you pray for that person over and over until you feel the contamination lift out of you. Some of you may need a bulldozer. You purpose to forgive, but you need another person to help you. And that's okay! Get the help you need. It's not an easy process.

It will take every ounce of emotional resolution you can muster. It will take the help of the Holy Spirit to pull you through, and it will take the help of a friend or pastor.

But what do you do about the person who harmed you? Remember that forgiving someone does not mean you go back to that person who has caused you harm. If someone is abusing you, you should not go back to the abuser. Remove yourself from their harmful ways. Block them from your life. Do not let them dump *more* harmful contamination into your life while you're trying to clean up their past offenses. Forgiveness does not mean you let the offender waltz back in. Nope—forgiveness is the way to become free from that person's harmful hold on your life.

Once we clean up the soil of our hearts, we need to be alert and attentive so our hearts stay clean and pure. We are not dumping grounds anymore!

I have learned this lesson. I have been dumped upon, sinned against, and betrayed. But I dug out the crud and I learned to forgive Christ's way, by praying for those who sinned against me. And then I freed myself of their hold over me. My ground is now clean, and I cannot begin to tell you of the joy and peace I now have. Christ's ways always work—for you and for me.

Prayer

Father God, I purpose to forgive the people who have hurt me in the past and the people who are hurting me now. I pray that their souls will find Your Son and their hearts will be transformed into Your image. I lay my pain at Your feet. Help me dig the bitterness out of my heart so I can spiritually build on good soil. Release me from the chains of un-forgiveness and help me to be supernaturally healed from the pain. Amen.

Be Honest

Let no unwholesome word proceed from your mouth,
but only such a word as is good for edification according to the
need of the moment, so that it will give grace to those who hear.
—EPHESIANS 4:29

AS A CHILD, I WAS PROFICIENT AT LYING. AS AN ADULT, I HAVE changed my ways. In relationships, however, I'm still not always honest for one simple reason: I cherish peaceful relationships so much that I often tell people what they want to hear just to keep my blessed serenity.

But it gets worse: This attitude has leaked into my relationship with God. I am not always honest with Him. If I'm worried, upset, hurting, or confused, I don't always tell Him. I don't want Him to think less of me or be disappointed in my attitude, and I really don't want to be disrespectful toward Him. I guess the bottom line is that sometimes I'm afraid to be honest with Him.

Honesty with God is our heart crying out to understand His character. Honesty with God is an open conversation about our doubts, our misunderstandings, our frustrations, and our inability to always understand His actions. It is us running to Him like a child runs to his father to get the answers to every question. Honesty in Father God is us trusting that He loves our questions and is willing to answer them.

I'm all for honesty in pursuit of understanding God, but some people think they're being honest with God when they're angry with Him. I don't agree, and I will even say that idea is spiritually dangerous and immature. Yes, we can honestly question God's actions, but we should never blame Him or be angry with Him for our circumstances, especially since our unfortunate circumstances are often our own doing. The real tragedy with being angry with God is that when we feel this way, our natural tendency is to turn away and erect walls.

The book of Psalms is filled with writings by people who poured out real emotions before the living God. They poured out fear, hurt, confusion, love, depression, anxiety, insecurities, hopelessness, and devotion. But they never poured out anger or disrespect. They knew He still loved them and accepted them as they were, even through their pain and uncertainty. They knew God was concerned with every part of their lives.

I want to be like the psalmists—willing and able to pour out my heart to God in confusion, hurt, and pain, as well as joy and pure love. I want to be honest with God about my emotions in an honoring, respectful, relationship-building way. I hope you do too.

Final Thoughts and Questions

Faith in God is not just mental; it's a private bond that touches and colors everything we are. Ask Him the hard questions. Be honest with Him in every area, because He already knows.

What are some of your questions about your life? Your areas of confusion and discouragement? Your hurts? Talk to Him about them. Ask Him the hard questions.

Prayer

Father, here I am before you. You know my faults, yet you love me even so. This knowledge overwhelms me and moves my soul with love back toward you. I lay before you all of my questions about you, my misconceptions of you, my confusion about you, and even my doubts of you. Shape me, mold me, teach me, and train me. Use me for your glory and transform these doubts and questions into a strong faith that resembles your Son's faith. Amen.

Be a Light

"You are the light of the world.
A city set on a hill cannot be hidden;
nor does anyone light a lamp and put it under a basket,
but on the lampstand, and it gives light to all
who are in the house. Let your light shine before men in such
a way that they may see your good works,
and glorify your Father who is in heaven."
—MATTHEW 5:14–16

DURING HANUKKAH—THE FESTIVAL OF LIGHTS—JEWS WOULD illuminate the temple with hundreds of candles and light a huge menorah that could be seen from many miles away. They would dance and pray and wait for the Messiah to come. Some modern scholars believe it was during this celebration that Jesus, the Messiah, stepped forward and declared, "I am the Light of the world" (John 8:12).

Somewhere between 167–160 BC, the Syrians, led by Antiochus, vented their anger on the Jews. They killed many of them, and the rest they forbade to worship. They defiled the temple of YAHWEH by dedicating it to the false god Zeus. To add insult to injury, on God's holy altar they sacrificed a pig, an animal not meant to be sacrificed or eaten according to God's laws (Lev. 11:1–47). Judah Maccabee, a zealous Jew, and his passionate followers revolted against this atrocity. They retook the temple, cleansed the altar, and started the rededication process. But they could find only one cruse of uncontaminated olive oil, which was essential for the rededication. The amount they found was enough for one day. The problem was that it took eight days to prepare new ceremonially acceptable oil. But a miracle occurred when that small quantity of oil continued to burn for eight days—thus the miracle of Hanukkah.

The menorah (candelabra) used for Hanukkah has nine branches to hold candles. The symbolic significance of this is beautiful. The middle candle of the nine is known as the servant candle; it is lit first and then used to light each of the other candles during this holiday. The other eight candles symbolize every believer, receiving his or her light from the Messiah, who is the servant candle—the Light of the world.

Jesus is not just *a* light; He is *the* Light. Light is truly remarkable. It's bright, you know where it comes from, and its rays are far reaching. Light makes darkness disappear, it shines on both the good and the evil, and it empowers all to see because it's available to everyone. Jesus is this type of light.

As Christ's disciples, it is our job to reflect Jesus's light to the world. Christ does not want us to run and hide from the world, but to confront it with His light. The world is dark from terrorism, wars, starvation, adultery, pornography, sexual abuse, physical and verbal abuse, greed, foul language, and oppression. But Jesus instructed us to, amid this terrible darkness, *shine brightly* and push back the darkness (Matt. 5:16 and Acts 13:47).

How did He shine His light? By helping the hurting. He set the spiritual prisoners free. He bound their wounds. He fed the hungry. He touched the unclean. He went against the grain and rocked the system. He showed us the Father's heart. He lived it. He preached it. He loved others while brightly beaming the Father's heart.

How can you and I live as children of the light today? We too can touch the hungry, the unclean, the homeless, the orphans, and the widows by meeting their needs and binding their wounds. We can help the hurting. We can set the spiritual prisoners free. We can show the world our Father's heart. We can preach it by living it.

Final Thoughts and Questions

Another way to be a light is to make it a daily practice to perform love deeds for others because of your love for God. Whether these love deeds are small or large, they are ways you can show the world you carry the light of Christ inside.

How can you be a light today? What love deeds can you perform? Keep your eyes open; opportunities are all around you.

Prayer

Father of Light, you are brilliant. Help my life shine in this dark world. Help me to shine like your beautiful Son. Show me ways that I can push back the darkness, and give me eyes to see ways that I can perform love deeds to those around me. Amen.

Day Forty-Nine

Daily Conversations

Answer me when I call, O God of my righteousness!
You have relieved me in my distress;
be gracious to me and hear my prayer.
—PSALM 4:1

HAVE YOU EVER HAD A ONE-SIDED CONVERSATION? YOU LISTEN while the other person talks and talks and talks. Irritating, isn't it? A healthy conversation is balanced. You talk, they listen. Then they talk, you listen.

Sometimes I feel my prayer time with the Lord is too often a one-sided, unhealthy, it's-all-about-me event. I talk and talk and talk some more, and He listens and listens—and perhaps He gets weary of my talking. He probably has some important things to say to me, but I can't hear because my lips are too busy flapping.

Prayer ought to be *balanced* conversations with God that allow our souls to connect to His. It is talking—*and* it's listening to what *He* is saying. It's a perfectly balanced communication and connection.

This type of connection can happen all day long without ending. It can be random, anytime-anywhere praise that says, "Wow, God. You sure painted a beautiful sunrise this morning." Or it can be a quick prayer asking for help while you're busy at work. Or it can be a prayer for direction, and then listening for the answer. This holy connection is for us to reap the rewards of a covenant relationship with God. Because Jesus is our eternal High Priest, we now can go before our Father and speak to Him directly. What a privilege! What an *honor*!

I believe Jesus is the perfect example of someone who prayed without ceasing, and that included listening to His Father's direction without ceasing. He prayed often, many times going off by Himself to talk to His Father. He prayed that the Father's will be accomplished. And He talked to God about everything. He knew time in prayer would align His desires with God's desires, and He knew His ministry depended on God's help.

And because Jesus is the perfect example for prayer, it's good that He taught us how to pray in Matthew 6:9–13 (KJV):

- **"Our Father"**—We are His children; He really is our true Father.

- **"Hallowed be thy name"**—His name is the most holy, and He deserves all worship and all awe!

- **"Thy kingdom come"**—We are to have a heavenly perspective when we pray. God's kingdom, not our earthly worries, must be our main focus.

- **"Thy will be done in earth, as it is in heaven"**—We desire only God's will for our lives, our world, and our eternity.

- **"Give us this day our daily bread"**—We recognize that He provides all our needs—always!

- **"Forgive us our debts, as we forgive our debtors"**—He wants us to genuinely repent of our sins and forgive those who have wronged us so He can forgive our sins.

- **"Lead us not into temptation, but deliver us from evil"**— God gives us the strength to overcome temptation and helps us overcome evil.

- **"For thine is the kingdom, and the power, and the glory, for ever."**—We long for an eternal kingdom full of all the power of heaven and earth, and filled with all glory forever and ever.

Prayer

Father, You are all-powerful and full of glory. Holy is Your name. May Your kingdom rule in my life. Give me eyes to see Your kingdom. Thank You for providing everything I need today and always. Deliver me from evil and temptation. I forgive all who have sinned against me. Thank You for forgiving me. Let me hear what You are saying today. Give me ears to hear. Amen.

When You Don't Feel Like Loving

*"Greater love has no one than this,
that one lay down his life for his friends."*
—JOHN 15:13

WE ALL GO THROUGH SEASONS IN OUR LIVES WHEN WE WOULD rather shut out the world than be part of it. But during these less-than-desirable periods we have the greatest potential of earning some awesome heavenly rewards. When we decide to love someone who isn't really lovable, that's a heavenly reward opportunity.

Loving when we don't feel like it is called *sacrificial love.* Christ is the perfect example of this type of love. He sacrificed His life for a world that cursed Him and spat in His face—not something that would make *me* feel loving.

My amazing parents have always been an example of sacrificial love. They raised seven children and opened their hearts and home to twelve more. As I was growing up, I slept on the couch for months at a time because my bedroom was occupied. We also ate in shifts because we didn't own enough plates and forks to go around (you would not believe the number of dishes that needed to be washed every day—by hand!).

I'm sure many days Mom and Dad questioned their sanity and wondered whether they were doing the right thing. I'm sure they sometimes wanted to quit, but they never did. In fact, they're still going strong today. At eighty-five and eighty-two years of age, they are *still* foster parents, as well as parents to a special-needs daughter they adopted from China. Theirs is not an easy job for anyone.

I have tried to be like my parents. I have tried to walk in their shoes. But I've got to say, it's tough! Changing Chernobyl diapers of babies that are not from my womb is so hard! Cleaning up the messes of others whom I barely know is maddening. Mothering, patiently teaching, or lovingly tickling children who are unruly and wild is beyond difficult. Selfless, sacrificial love is possible only with strong dedication to the transformation process—*and* with some major help from the Holy Spirit.

Sometimes showing mercy and kindness comes easily. We get a warm feeling in our guts when we help someone in distress. When we're asked for more than just our "spare change," however, sacrifice becomes difficult. When we're asked to give away our cloaks or go the extra mile, those are big sacrifices. All the warm, fuzzy feelings leave! But Jesus tells us to show this kind of love to everyone, *especially* when it's tough, because that's how things are done in His kingdom.

Final Thoughts and Questions

When you love others by sacrificing, you're truly becoming transformed into Christ's image. And this is what the whole remodeling process is all about—becoming more like Him. How strong or weak are you at sacrificial love? Rate yourself. How can you love sacrificially? Write down areas where you can help others today—even though it costs you much.

Prayer

Father, bring to my mind how I can show sacrificial love today. Open my eyes to see the needs of others and give me a heart of compassion to step out and show love, even when it's hard. Send me the help of the Holy Spirit to help me as I go out and serve. Help me to become completely transformed into the image of Jesus Christ today. Amen.

Day Fifty-One

The Kingdom Perspective

The seventh angel blew his trumpet,
and there were loud voices in heaven, saying,
"The kingdom of the world has become
the kingdom of our Lord and of his Christ,
and he shall reign for ever and ever.
—REVELATION 11:15 RSV

I RECENTLY WATCHED SEVERAL YOUTUBE VIDEOS OF PEOPLE WHO have died, gone to heaven, and then come back to life. It's amazing how their stories resemble all the others. They all say they saw a bright light, they felt engulfed in a complete sense of love, they saw and even talked to many family members who have passed, and then they were told they needed to go back. When these people tell their profound stories, they all start crying when they talk about the love they felt from Jesus. Many of them go on to say they felt as if this earthly life is just a dream, while heaven felt more real.

You could say their perspectives have been altered; they are now kingdom-minded individuals. They are no longer afraid of death because they look forward to the end of this life and the beginning of the next.

We all need our perspectives altered to become kingdom-minded individuals like these folks. Our perception, like theirs, should be that this world is just a dream we are passing through, and when we wake up in heaven, we will be back in the real world where our souls were first created so long ago.

Jesus spoke often about God's kingdom. He seemed to believe that kingdom thinking is highly important. And from the way He taught in His parables, His kingdom was spiritual in nature.

He said things like:

- If you want to be great in God's kingdom, become a servant to all (Matt. 20:26).

- Seek first His kingdom and all things will be given to you (Matt. 6:33).

- The kingdom is like a mustard seed, the smallest of seeds, yet "when it is full grown, it is larger than the garden plants and becomes a tree, so that the birds of the air come and nest in its branches" (Matt. 13:32).

- God's kingdom is in your midst (Luke 17:21).

- His kingdom is not of this world (John 18:36).

- "The kingdom of God is not eating and drinking, but righteousness and peace and joy in the Holy Spirit" (Rom. 14:17).

- "The time is fulfilled, and the kingdom of God is at hand; repent and believe in the gospel" (Mark 1:15).

God's kingdom is the opposite of the way we think. It's upside-down thinking. That's why we need our thinking altered; kingdom thinking does not come naturally. Jesus tells us what we must do to enter His kingdom—be born again.

When our eyes are opened and we finally understand what it means to have the kingdom of God inside of us, our lives will never be the same. His kingdom is full of love, light, and authority. When we allow Father's kingdom to live in us, we start to love all humanity, we shine so brightly that darkness is pushed back, and we learn to walk in its full authority. God's kingdom is so powerful and strong that it has complete authority over everything! Cancer cells must melt in its presence, other diseases must disappear, and evil must flee because of its power. Not only are we the temple of God, but we are bearing forth His kingdom. We are His warriors!

God's kingdom is also physical. When we look at how God interacted with mankind in the garden, we can surmise that it was always His desire to be in a loving partnership with all of His creation—plant, animal, and human. He wanted to live here with us and fellowship daily. But sin arrived and spoiled God's plan. Even worse, after the fall, mankind was in partnership with Satan! It was now up to God to conquer him.

And He did just that. He conquered the Enemy by sending His Son to live, die, and redeem us so we could be reconciled with God. He ensured that final victory in the glorious resurrection of Jesus the Messiah.

For two thousand years God has waited for the moment when He will send His Son back here. When He does, Christ will restore this earth to the wonderful kingdom He always wanted for us and with us. When Jesus comes again, He will set up His kingdom and reign over a renewed, restored world, a world where we can have face-to-face fellowship for all eternity. I long for that time. Even nature longs for that time! The whole earth groans under the weight of sin and looks forward to the reign of the King.

We can enter that spiritual kingdom today by becoming born again, becoming a disciple, and living like Jesus taught us. At the same time, we can look forward to His physical kingdom. Soon, real soon, God's kingdom will come. Our Savior, Jesus Christ the Messiah and King, will rule and reign forever!

Final Thoughts and Questions

Look for ways to be kingdom-minded: be last, be least, and be a servant. Look for ways to help others. Look for ways to live out His spiritual instructions as though you are already living in God's physical kingdom.

Prayer

Father, give me spiritual eyes to see ways I can live out Christ's spiritual instructions on kingdom living. Give me strength to be last and least. Help me to be a servant to all. Get me ready for Your physical kingdom. May Your kingdom come today in my life, and in my family, and in my world. I love You. Amen.

Day Fifty-Two

Apply Kingdom Thinking to Your Faith

Immediately the boy's father cried out and said,
"I do believe; help my unbelief."
—MARK 9:24

THIS TRUE STORY TOOK PLACE IN ISRAEL, AS TOLD IN MARK 9:14–29.

A distraught father brings his mute and demonically possessed son to Jesus. But when the son sees Jesus, the evil spirit throws the boy into a convulsion. He falls and foams at the mouth.

"How long has this been happening to your son?" Jesus asks.

"Since childhood," the troubled father answers. "It has often thrown him into the fire and into water to destroy him. If you can do anything, take pity on us and help us."

"If I can? All things are possible to him who believes," Jesus replies.

"I do believe—please help my unbelief," the father says.

Then Jesus reaches out, rebukes the evil spirit, and completely heals the boy.

Can you imagine the desperation of this father? He had faith in the Healer, but he had spent many years seeing firsthand the reality of evil. That evil was too real, too powerful. His son's problem was this father's concern every waking moment and probably his final thought every night. He believed in the healing power of God, but he was also dealing with his unbelief.

I think we all can relate. Everyone has doubts about God at some point. I have struggled with various God issues on and off for years.

It's hard to admit to that; I'm afraid it makes me look like a woman of weak faith.

But this story in Mark 9 shows us it's okay to tell God we're struggling with an element of unbelief. It's okay to ask for His help. In fact, I think it's possible to let our faith doubts become faith builders, not faith killers—but only when they cause us to dig to find the true answers.

Father God is more than able to handle our tough questions. He wants us to acknowledge them and bring them before Him because He is eager to show us His truths. His truths are what set us free.

Here's a list of questions about God that I and others have struggled with. After each question is a biblical answer.

- **Is the Word of God true? Does it represent all truth?** "All Scripture is God-breathed and is useful for teaching, rebuking, correcting and training in righteousness" (2 Tim. 3:16 NIV).

- **Does God have a plan for my life?** "Indeed, the very hairs of your head are all numbered" (Luke 12:7).

- **Is God the only god?** "You were shown these things so that you might know that the LORD is God; beside him there is no other" (Deut. 4:35 NIV).

- **Is Jesus really the Son of God?** "A voice from heaven said, 'This is my Son, whom I love; with him I am well pleased'" (Matt. 3:17 NIV).

- **Does heaven really exist?** "[He] showed me the holy city, Jerusalem, coming down out of heaven from God.... Her brilliance was like a very costly stone, as a stone of crystal-clear jasper. It had a great and high wall, with twelve gates, and at the gates twelve angels;... The material of the wall was jasper; and the city was pure gold, like clear glass" (Rev. 21:10–18).

- **How can a loving God allow bad things to happen?** The wickedness in this world not only breaks God's heart, but He hates it and hates what it does to us, His children. Satan is the one to blame for evil. But when we surrender our lives to God, He can take what Satan has meant for evil and turn it into something good. "We know that in all things God works for the good of those who love him, who have been called according to his purpose" (Rom. 8:28 NIV).

- **What is the litmus test that proves God exists?** The litmus test is the peaceful presence of the Holy Spirit in our souls; the peace we can have even amid chaos. "You will experience God's peace, which exceeds anything we can understand" (Phil. 4:7 NLT).

- **Why doesn't God answer my prayers?** Sometimes God doesn't answer our prayers the way we asked him to answer them. If our motives are not pure, God will not answer (James 4:3). If we have unconfessed known sin in our hearts, He will not answer (Ps. 66:18). Or sometimes the timing is not right (Luke 18:1).

Final Thoughts and Questions

The next time you wonder if God is in control, remember this truth about Him: He is the Most High. The next time you worry about life, remember that He is trustworthy as your provider. The next time life sends you trouble, remember that God is compassionate and desires to help you through the fire. When you are faced with financial trouble, remember that God owns the cattle on a thousand hills (Ps. 50:10). When temptation raises its ugly head, remember that He has given you a way out, because He wants you to walk blameless before Him.

When life gets messy, remember who He is. *He is the truth!*

Prayer

Father, I do believe—please help me through times of unbelief. Help my sometimes shaky faith to grow into an unmovable mountain. Here is my heart—I trust in You alone. Here is my faith—help it to grow. I love You and thank You that You love me and want me to mature in my faith. Amen.

Day Fifty-Three

Apply Kingdom Thinking to Your Job

"Do not worry then, saying, 'What will we eat?' or
'What will we drink?' or 'What will we wear . . . ?'
. . . your heavenly Father knows that you need all these things.
But seek first His kingdom and His righteousness,
and all these things will be added to you."
—MATTHEW 6:31–33

ONE OF THE MOST CHALLENGING THINGS ABOUT BEING A DISCIPLE of Jesus is taking our faith with us wherever we go. And for most of us, one of the hardest places to take our faith is the workplace. Since a job is all about making enough money to take care of the family, we tend to divorce our performance on the job from our faith and justify questionable actions:

"Bobby needs braces, so I have to be ruthless to get the order."

"I deserve this promotion more than everyone else; therefore it won't hurt if the boss knows this juicy information about my coworker."

"Everybody backstabs. After all, it's not personal; it's just business."

Sometimes we fight dirty as we climb that corporate ladder. Sometimes we gossip and slander to make ourselves look better than the next guy. It's so easy to fall into this trap, especially when we see others doing it.

Other workplace issues can include lying to cover our tracks, blaming others for our own mistakes, and intra-office flirting. The temptations and forces at work against us in the workplace are tremendous, but God is calling us to rise above it all.

Those of you who work at home have challenges as well. Take soap operas, for instance. Do they have the kind of content your spirit is likely to find edifying? What about misbehaving children who push you beyond frustration? Or online temptations? These homebound pressures are as hard as any other workplace temptation.

According to Matthew 6:31–33, we are not to worry about or engage in these job-related stresses. We are not to worry about what to eat or drink or how to clothe ourselves (things we work hard to provide). Instead we are to be first concerned about God's kingdom. And when His kingdom becomes our top priority, everything else falls into place. God supplies our food, drink, clothes, car payments, rent or mortgage payments, and everything else we struggle to provide. He takes care of it all.

Living out God's kingdom in our workplaces means we stop being ruthless and stop scrapping for every dollar. God will provide for Bobby's braces. We can stop fudging numbers or fighting our way up the ladder. We can just work hard and honestly and let God supply every need, as He has promised to do.

We *can* act like Jesus in our workplace. We *can* live out His truths in our workplace. We *can* let our actions *and reactions* reflect Christ's actions and reactions. We can honestly say, "I want what is best for my boss and my coworkers. I want them to be blessed. I want for them everything good," so that at the end of the day we can go to sleep with a clear conscience, knowing we were good disciples.

Final Thoughts and Questions

Living the truth in the workplace does not mean you go in there brandishing your Bible, slashing the sinners to shreds. It means you choose not to partake of the garbage. When gossip starts, you say only positive words about the "gossipee." When untruth is spoken, you counter with a truth. You try to connect with others where they are to show them Christ's love. You stay faithful to your husband and your family when faced with the temptation to flirt. You shine God's light in a positive way that makes following Christ attractive to the unbeliever.

Your job is to change your little world one soul at a time, from adult coworkers to your own small children.

Prayer

Father, give me wisdom and strength to overcome job-related stresses and temptations. Help me to be a light in my workplace, and help me to touch my coworkers' lives with Your great love and light. Amen.

PHASE
SIX

Build through Good and Bad Weather

Into every life a little bad weather falls—perhaps marital disunity, rebellious children, or financial pressures. As spiritual remodelers, we must weather these storms and labor to build a better spiritual life. Sometimes we must batten down the hatches and ride it out; other times we must fight our way through. Spiritually, we must call out to God for help, reacting and responding like Christ and hanging on to God's promises with white knuckles.

He is our way through the storms! The winds and the waves must obey Him and cease. They did in the past, and they will for your storms as well.

Finding Courage in Christ's Example

God has not given us a spirit of fear and timidity,
but of power, love, and self-discipline.
—2 TIMOTHY 1:7 NLT

I'M DEATHLY AFRAID OF MICE. WHEN I SEE A MOUSE, I RELEASE A primordial scream of such high decibel that it is sometimes mistaken for a tornado siren going off right next to the ears. Loud! Painful! Shrill! As I'm screaming and doing the panicked crazy-lady jig on top of a table, I look for a weapon to protect myself. There are never any good weapons on tabletops! The continued screaming and the jig combined with utter and complete terror leaves me breathless and light-headed. If the mouse doesn't kill me, my hyperventilating will.

Fear is powerful. It makes us behave irrationally with a merciless choke hold that does not let go. And sometimes it makes us look ridiculous, leaving us horribly embarrassed!

We women face a lot of fears, some of us rodents and creatures with eight hairy legs. But we can also be afraid of failure, disapproval, someone hurting our children, terrorism, economic hardships, and loneliness. We can tend to let fear control our thoughts, actions, and conversations. It can rule us.

Right before the children of Israel were preparing to cross the Jordan River into the Promised Land, God told Joshua, "Be strong and courageous. Do not be afraid; do not be discouraged, for the LORD your God will be with you wherever you go" (Josh. 1:9 NIV).

Three times God told Joshua to be strong and courageous. Three times He told him to remember that He was going with them.

Physically, Joshua had much to fear. Remember, giants in the land wanted to squish them. He also faced violent kingdoms, idol worship, vicious animals, and evil of every sort. I guess that's why God had to remind him three times not to fear.

I know we don't face physical giants in our lives today, but we do face giants of other types. We face the giants of a dissolving marriage, rebellious children, cancers and other diseases, evil people wanting to harm us in any way they can, financial ruin, loneliness, and lack of connection. God wants us to face down these giants.

Where do we find the courage to stand up to them? I believe it starts in our minds, our battlegrounds. It starts when we confront negative, spineless thoughts and turn them into courageously strong thoughts. Instead of saying, "I can't," in its place we can say, "With God all things are possible" (see Phil. 4:13).

Having courageous thoughts stem from knowing our Defender. Joshua saw firsthand the cloud by day and the pillar of fire by night. He saw firsthand water that sprang up out of a rock and manna supplied every morning. He saw the hand of God move in miraculous ways. His faith in his Defender was great. Yet even he had to be reminded not to fear. He purposed to remember those times of miracles, and he used them as courage builders to fight the fear.

Are we like Joshua? Do we know our Defender? Have we seen Him display miracles in our lives? Have we seen Him display miracles in others' lives? Do we let these miracles build our courage and faith?

As we take steps to conquer fear, it's sometimes easier to tackle the smaller fears before we face the big ones. Jesus trained His disciples on smaller issues before they faced big ones. His first miracles had to do with multiplying food (wine, fish, and loaves) before He healed the lepers and the blind.

What smaller giants can you start to face down today? Fear of confrontation or fear of failure? Whatever it is, remember what God told

Joshua: "Don't be afraid because I am going with you!" The Almighty is with us just as He was with Joshua. He is our Defender and our strength!

Final Thoughts and Questions

Read stories from the Old Testament and the New that will build your faith and courage.

- For courage to fight the *giant of disease* read Mark 5:21–34.

- For courage to fight the *giant of rebellious children* read Luke 15:11–32, the story of the prodigal son.

- For courage to fight the *giant of a failing marriage* read Ephesians 5:22–33.

- Also read the stories of old: David slaying Goliath (1 Sam. 17), Joshua and the walls of Jericho (Josh. 6), the Passover story (Ex. 12), how God protected baby Jesus from Herod (Matt. 2), God's provision for the children of Israel throughout the wilderness (Ex. 16), Queen Esther (Est. 1–2), Ruth and Naomi (entire book of Ruth), and so many more. The Bible is chock-full of amazing stories that show the mighty hand of our Great Defender—YAHWEH Almighty!

Prayer

Father, give me courage to tackle my fears today. Help me take on the smaller ones so that later I will be able to face and conquer my biggest fears. I am determined to put my trust in You concerning the things that cause me to fear. Help me to be strong and of good courage. Help me to remember that You are going with me! Amen.

Day Fifty-Five

Keep an Eye on Each Other— Intercessory Prayer

Our struggle is not against flesh and blood,
but against the rulers, against the powers,
against the world forces of this darkness,
against the spiritual forces
of wickedness in the heavenly places.
—EPHESIANS 6:12

HOW MANY PEOPLE DO YOU KNOW WHO ARE STRUGGLING RIGHT now? Some are struggling in their finances, or emotions, or marriages. Some are struggling physically, or mentally, or are carrying a personal burden too big to carry alone. You probably know many. I know many. But too often I've told someone I'll pray for them and neglected to follow through. I'm sure I'm not the only one. We seem to have forgotten how to stand in the gap and keep an eye on each other.

Intercessory prayer is the process of being an advocate for people, standing up for them and persistently pleading their case. In a sense, you're handcuffing yourself to the people in need—making their burdens your burdens, making their pain your pain, and making their cries to God your cries to God.

In the Old Testament, the high priest was the only one allowed to go behind the veil into the holy of holies where the Spirit of God dwelled. In this holy place he would plead for the forgiveness of the nation of Israel. Similarly, Jesus is our High Priest from the heavenly,

182

priestly order of Melchizedek (Heb. 5:10). He goes into the heavenly holy of holies before Father and pleads for you and for me, making Him the perfect example of intercession.

Another beautiful example of intercession is Simon of Cyrene. As Jesus carried the cross up Calvary's hill, the burden was more than He could physically manage. Jesus's earthly body was giving out, so Simon of Cyrene stepped in and bore the cross for Him. He bore the burden Jesus could no longer bear alone. This example is a beautiful picture of intercessory prayer. We see the need and step in to bear the burden of another. We carry that burden up the mountain to God.

Final Thoughts and Questions

Whom do you know who has been carrying a heavy burden? How can you pray for that person? How can you make his or her burdens your burdens? Maybe you'll want to create a prayer journal to better keep track of all the people you know who need special prayer. Add to the list as more needs come to your attention, and then designate one or two days a week to specifically lift up to God those in your journal.

Prayer

Oh, Holy One, bring to my mind those in my life who are in need of prayer or a helping hand. Give me creative ideas on how I can help. I ask that you touch these ones with your love, healing, deliverance, and your deep profound joy. And help me to be a vessel to reach these hurting ones in Your Name. Amen.

An Active Faith

Without faith it is impossible to please Him,
for he who comes to God must believe that He is
and that He is a rewarder of those who seek Him.
—HEBREWS 11:6

BEING CHRIST'S DISCIPLE IS NO EASY TASK. IT'S A LIFE FULL OF SELFless surrender, serving, and fighting our natural tendencies. It's an *active* life, full of *active* faith with nothing passive about it. A passive faith says, "It's enough to just believe." But James tells us in James 2:19 that "even the demons believe—and tremble" (NKJV). That tells me our faith must be more than a belief; it must be alive and kicking.

Discipleship is an action word. It's *being like* Jesus in everything we say and do. Discipleship is an action just as love is an action, *showing* others we love them by *meeting* their needs before we meet our own. So too faith is an action, *living* our belief in God through our discipleship to Jesus.

Hebrews 11 tells us what active faith looks like. Abel *offered* his best sacrifice. Enoch *pleased* God. Noah *built* an ark. Abraham *obeyed* and *left* his home before he received his inheritance. Joshua and the Israelites had to *march* around Jericho and *shout* with a great shout before God's power was activated, causing the walls to fall. Moses *left* Egypt. Rahab *hid* the spies. Christ *obeyed* His Father and *offered* Himself on the cross. The crippled man's friends had to *tear* a hole in the roof and *lower* him down to Christ before he could be healed. I imagine Christ felt proud of their active faith. They put their muscles and their energy behind their belief.

A faith full of action starts with the words coming out of our mouths. When life gets ugly, what are we saying? Are we admitting defeat, filled with doom and gloom? Or are we declaring victory? Our words can either defeat us or lead us into greater faith and awesome victory.

Our words of faithful confession increase our faith; we believe everything He said. Our faithful confessions say, "I can do all things through him who gives me strength" (Phil. 4:13 NIV); we believe it because He said so! On the other hand, the opposite is true; a negative confession is the fruit of negative thinking. But when we get our thinking lined up with God's Word *and* His promises, our faith comes alive. It moves from passive to active.

Christ preached an active faith and rewarded people by saying, "Your faith has made you well; go in peace" (Mark 5:34). That's what I want for me. That's what I want for you. Your faith has made you well; go in peace.

Final Thoughts and Questions

- Is your faith active? Are you living it out?

- In what areas are you successfully living out your faith, and in what areas do you need to improve?

Prayer

Father, help my faith to be more active daily. Help me make my words declare Your victory. Help my faith be alive and active, a reflection of my trust in You. Amen.

Day Fifty-Seven

Draw Near

Draw near to God and
He will draw near to you.
—JAMES 4:8

IMAGINE YOURSELF IN THE MIDDLE OF A FAST-MOVING RIVER. YOU'RE being swept downstream, and the cold water is stinging your eyes and numbing your hands and feet. The claws of tree roots grab at your clothes and pull you under. You're drowning and desperate for help. Your lungs ache for a deep breath as you are pulled under yet again.

Now picture God, standing on the shore and throwing you a lifeline. You grab the rope and hang on. But that's not enough. The rope isn't keeping you above water; it's just keeping you from floating farther downstream. It isn't until you hand-over-hand along the rope that you start moving toward the shore. Now picture God hand-overhanding it too, pulling you in. With every move you make, He makes a move too, pulling you closer. You and God work together until you make it safely back to shore and are in His arms.

We are often caught in the river of life, flowing helplessly downstream. Life's storms are washing us away, and we face the real possibility of drowning. But our amazing Father and His holy Son stand on the shore, throwing us a lifeline. It's up to us to grab that lifeline. It's up to us to hand-over-hand that lifeline to safety, to Him. It's up to us to draw near to God.

I love the story in Mark 5:25–34 about the woman who suffered with an issue of blood. She saw the lifeline, grabbed it, and drew near to safety. She knew how to draw near to her Healer even though life's storm was washing her away. It's the story of a sick, "unclean" woman who spent all she had seeking traditional help through doctors and medicine until she finally ran out of money and options. Then one day she heard about Jesus the Healer, who was coming to her town.

When He arrived, the crowds gathered, and so did she. The crowds pressed in to see Him, and so did she. Suddenly a man appeared at Jesus's side, begging Him to go to his house to heal his daughter. Jesus replied, "Take me to her," and He turned to leave. Tragically, someone had beaten our gal to her healing!

But she didn't give up. This was the lifeline she desperately needed, and she held on. She reached out and touched the healer's hem. Now, the "hem" we read about in the Bible is not the lowest part of Jesus's robe, where the rough edge is hemmed up, but the tassels on the corners of His garment, which were also called "wings." Our desperate woman not only had faith in this healer, but she had faith that He was the promised Messiah. She was probably familiar with Malachi 4:2, "But for you who fear My name, the sun of righteousness will rise with healing in its wings," which is a prophecy about the Messiah. The woman's faith and her actions not only allowed her to receive her healing, they also declared Jesus as the Messiah. Her "drawing near" declared loudly, *This man is the promised Messiah!*

I can't help but admire this amazing woman.

Each one of us has issues keeping us from using our lifeline effectively. They keep us merely hanging on in the middle of the fast-moving river, still fighting the current, in danger of drowning, still struggling for life instead of hand-over-handing our lifeline to safety. God wants us to name those issues so He can heal them.

Final Thoughts and Questions

What are your issues? Are you afraid of turning over control? Of letting your guard down? Maybe you're too timid to grab hold of that lifeline and start pulling for all you're worth. Maybe you're satisfied with the status quo. Maybe you tell yourself your sickness or problem isn't so bad, that many others have it much worse.

Precious daughter of God, grab hold of that lifeline and start pulling yourself toward your Savior! Let Him release the power of God into your heart, life, status quo, circumstances, sickness, family, troubles, and day-to-day living. Then let His peace fill you and heal you! Remember Christ's words to our heroine: "Daughter, your faith has healed you. Go in peace" (Mark 5:34 NIV).

Prayer

Father, I grab onto your lifeline. I purposely draw nearer to you. Thank you for your Son who has come to me with healing in His wings. Thank you that you love me so much that you always throw me that lifeline. Thank you that you never leave me stranded in this fast-moving, dangerous life, but instead are always on the shore trying to save me. I love you and I thank you. Amen.

Dress for the Weather

For though I am free from all men,
I have made myself a slave to all, so that I may win more.
To the Jews I became as a Jew, so that I might win Jews;
to those who are under the Law, [I became] as under the Law ...
that I might win those who are under the Law;
to those who are without law, as without law ...
that I might win those who are without law.
To the weak I become weak, that I might win the weak;
I have become all things to all men,
so that I may by all means save some.
I do all things for the sake of the gospel,
so that I may become a fellow partaker of it.
—1 CORINTHIANS 9:19–23

As a builder who works mostly outside, in the winter I dress warmly to ward off frostbite. And because I really, really, really hate to be cold. But when summer's scorching sun is shining down, I had better not still be wearing my long johns or I will perish in the heat.

Brother Paul told us something analogous: "I have become all things to all men, that I may by all means save some" (1 Cor. 9:22). Dressing for the weather—or in this case, dressing for our culture—is the unselfish act of becoming all things to all people so that we might win some for Christ.

When people don't believe as I do, either spiritually or politically, I can get hot under the collar. I must bite my tongue to avoid saying something I'll regret later. I'm trying hard to be more compassionate with those who differ from me on topics I'm fiercely passionate about. I'm trying to be more relatable in this area, to be all things to all people.

People hear the message of Christ better when they know the communicator can relate to their circumstances—and doesn't snarl at them. I need to be compassionate and in touch with whom I'm trying to reach. Instead of staying stuck in my quaint little hyper-Christian subculture where nonbelievers are not welcome, I need to reach out with welcoming arms to the thieves, drug addicts, prostitutes, radical leftists, educated, uneducated, homeless, homosexuals, rich, poor— every culture and subculture—so that *all* can hear the gospel and grasp its meaning. I need to take Jesus to them.

Jesus reached out and touched every type of hurting. He went to the tax collectors, the unclean, the demon possessed, and adulterers. He went to the ones who were sick, and He took to them a message of love and redemption. His genuine love and wisdom drew them in. He didn't shut Himself off from the outside. He was always moved with compassion toward the masses and continuously reached out to every culture and subculture.

Five times Paul tells us in 1 Corinthians 9 that his aim in acclimating to the way people live is to win them. Then in verse 22 he says, "I have become all things to all men, so that I may by all means save some." Five times it was to "win" people; in verse 22 it is to "save" people. Then verse 23 gives one last aim: "I do all things for the sake of the gospel, so that I may become a fellow partaker of it."

Our goal, like his, should be to do all things for the sake of the gospel, to save the lost and to win the lost so that we can be partakers of the gospel. That is what I want for me. I can't say I'm great at it, but I am working on it. I'm a small-town, raised-in-the-Midwest country girl, and some people scare me. The overly tattooed, scantily dressed, leather clad, motorcycle riding people are not people I would naturally choose to hang out with. They intimidate me! But if we are to be as

Paul encourages us to be, we must break out of our comfort zones to reach the hurting and even the scary.

God's net is wide. Christ wants us to bring the message of salvation to everyone. We need to keep dressing for the "current weather conditions" by going where God sends us, connecting with people outside of our cliques, and being all things to *all* people.

Final Thoughts and Questions

To whom outside of your comfort zone can you reach out to today? How can you take them the gospel to save and win them for Christ?

Prayer

Father, direct my steps to those people who are searching for and are ready to receive Your good news. Direct me to people outside of my comfort zone. Let me feel Your heart of love for those who are lost and wandering in darkness. Be a light inside me. Help me shine like Jesus! Amen.

Day Fifty-Nine

Be Diligent

[Do not be] lagging behind in diligence,
[but] fervent in spirit, serving the Lord.
—ROMANS 12:11

I'M THE WORST MONEY MANAGER OF ALL TIME! I BOUNCE CHECKS, run out of money in my account, and I am constantly in a money-worried state of mind. I am money impaired! My husband has cruelly kicked me off our account and set me up on my own. I think it's either his way of getting even with me or of trying to teach me some form of money management. So far? Zero success. This is one of my biggest challenges. I need to learn financial diligence.

Diligence is a mysterious godly trait, one we don't hear about too often. It means many things, but can be summed up the best by showing its opposite. Diligence is the opposite of laziness and neglect. It is, in a sense, doing today what I could have put off until tomorrow.

God does not want us lazy in our earthly work, finances included. "Whatever you do, work at it with all your heart, as working for the Lord, not for human masters" (Col. 3:23 NIV). He doesn't want us lazy in our spiritual work either. "Stand firm. Let nothing move you. Always give yourselves fully to the work of the Lord, because you know that your labor in the Lord is not in vain" (1 Cor. 15:58 NIV). We are to do all these things with gusto! As if we are doing them for the Lord, because we really are, whether or not we like it.

Here's a summary of Jesus's story of the talents (Matt. 25:14–30): A master gives talents to three different servants. He then goes away on a trip. The servant given five talents invests it to make five more talents. The servant given two talents invests it to make two more talents. But the servant given just one talent is lazy and uses fear to justify his laziness. He decides to hide the talent in the ground. When the master returns, he praises the two who increased their talents, but is angry and reprimands the lazy servant. In the end, the master takes away the lazy servant's talent and gives it to the one who has the most.

This story is a lesson in diligence. We are to take the finances, the blessings, and the spiritual gifts God has given us and use them for His glory, nurture them so they increase, and guard them so they are not taken away. We are not to bury them in the ground and lazily ignore them.

Let us faithfully practice diligence in every aspect of our lives! Because when we invest our finances, our talents, and our spiritual gifts for God, God makes sure they multiply.

Final Thoughts and Questions

- How are you at practicing diligence?
- How can you diligently use your finances, gifts, and talents to build God's kingdom?

Prayer

Father, help me to guard against spiritual laziness, physical laziness, and mental laziness. Help me to use all the gifts You've given me to build Your kingdom here on earth. Amen.

I Don't Understand— Why Me?

Consider it all joy, my brethren,
when you encounter various trials,
knowing that the testing
of your faith produces endurance.
—JAMES 1:2–3

HAVE YOU EVER HAD ONE OF THOSE DAYS WHEN EVERYTHING GOES wrong? I had one not too long ago.

I wake up with a migraine. Then my stomach takes a turn for the worse. "Great. Not only is my head pounding but I might just throw up too," I say to Tony. I'm miserable, but I get dressed and go to work anyway. The day creeps along at a snail's pace, but at least I'm surviving and doing my best to keep a good attitude.

After lunch, all hades lets loose. The house we're building sits on a three-foot-high foundation wall, and at this stage of construction only the subfloor is in place and only a few of the outside perimeter walls are built. The bad thing about not having all the outside walls up is that when you're in a hurry, it's easy to forget where the floor ends and the ground begins. In my rush, I walk off the subfloor and land in a heap. Cringing, I brush myself off, remove the gravel from where my elbow should be, and head to the toolbox to get whatever it was I was going after.

Still not paying attention to my feet, I step into a hole and twist my ankle. At this point my ankle hurts, my guts are rumbling, and my head is throbbing. I feel overwhelmed, but still I hold it together. I don't want to cry in front of a bunch of guys.

When I'm able, I get up from where I'm nursing my wounds and head back to work. Back on the subfloor, I look up and notice a board loosely nailed above my head, where it should not be. I pull on it hard and it suddenly gives way. Of course, it crashes down *hard* on my already smarting head.

That's the one that breaks the dam. I get angry. I start to cry. Everything on my body is aching and throbbing. I'm ready to turn in my resignation, but I can't because I'm part owner of this business, which only makes me cry harder!

We've all had days like that, when we encounter many small-ish trials, from relationship breakdowns to vehicle breakdowns. From uncomfortable nausea to painful migraines. Everyone gets zapped by these annoyances. They're totally impartial, happen at the most inconvenient times, and aren't fun! But one good thing about these little frustrations is they give us the opportunity to do some spiritual remodeling.

While it's true we have no control over the *whys* and *hows* of our particular trials, we do have control over our responses to them. Our reactions reflect and determine our spiritual growth—or lack thereof. When James told us to "consider it all joy" (James 1:2), he knew joy would *not* be our natural response. Our natural responses are more likely anger, complaining, and even bitterness. James knew this joy response had to be learned, a conscious choice. According to James, joy is not the absence of pain; real joy is a profound contentment that comes from knowing God is sovereign and in control of our lives. Wow!

When we stay faithful to God through these everyday trials, we are prepared for when the big doozies happen. Our faith will be solid, strong, and able to endure to the end. It will help us look at these smaller everyday trials as training for the big trials. After all, you can't run the Boston Marathon from start to finish without having first trained thoroughly by running many smaller races.

The Bible is full of stories of men and women who kept their faith strong through the smaller trials so when the big trials and tragedies came into their lives, they stayed true to God and received their reward in His kingdom. Consider Moses. His smaller trial—fleeing from Egypt—prepared him for the bigger trial of leading the entire nation of Israel out of Egypt (not to mention taking care of thousands of grumbling refugees on the trek across a grueling desert).

We must take life one trial at a time, fight against our natural responses, and cling to the supernatural joy responses. Instead of saying "Why me?" say "Why not me?"

Final Thoughts and Questions

- What situations you're facing today challenge your joy responses?

- With what practical ways can you change a defeated attitude into a positive attitude? An attitude that says, "I know this challenge is making me a better person."

Prayer

Father, help me to remember to consider it a joy when I face life's trials. Help me to act and react like Christ did when life became a trial for Him. Thank you that my trials build godly character and help me to spiritually mature. Amen.

Day Sixty-One

Triumph through Tragedy

We know that God causes all things
to work together for good to those who love God,
to those who are called according to His purpose.
—ROMANS 8:28

TRAGEDIES HAPPEN TO EVERYONE. SOME ARE BROUGHT ON BY OUR own actions, but others, such as personal debilitating illness, injustice, or the death of a loved one come out of the blue, blindside us, and leave us in pain and anguish. They often leave us doubting God's love for us or His sovereignty over our lives.

Yes, tragedies are severe, but we as believers can take comfort that they are not forever. We can find reassurance as we experience them by realizing that God feels our pain, He weeps with us and walks through the dark valley with us, holding tightly to our hands. He never leaves us alone in our pain!

Joseph of the Old Testament was a man well acquainted with tragedy. When he was a young boy, his jealous brothers sold him to a passing Egyptian caravan. As a slave in Egypt, he was falsely accused and thrown into prison. For seventeen long years his life was filled with anguish, yet he remained faithful to God and continued to live righteously. Because he stayed faithful to the Almighty, he was eventually released from jail and made second in command over all of Egypt. He went from rags to riches, from a stinky prison cell to the royal courts.

Years later, when Joseph finally met with his brothers, he offered forgiveness instead of seeking revenge. He said to them, "You mean evil against me, but God meant it for good" (Gen. 50:20). Through all the years of pain, Joseph chose to see God's sovereign hand moving in his life, even in prison and even through tragedies. It was a decision based on his knowledge and his faith in God.

Evil people do evil things. But when we surrender our will to God's will, He is always in control. When we remain faithful, pliable, and obedient to God, He turns evil into something good that will benefit all. He turns our tragedies into triumphs! To me, this is one of the greatest perks of being Jesus Christ's disciple.

The alternatives to remaining faithful to God through our hardships are not pleasant. Either we deny that God is good and believe He has caused our pain out of spite, or we deny that God is all-powerful, and therefore He is not able to prevent our suffering. In the end, both of these ways lead us to abandon our faith in God, and that is the *real* tragedy.

Final Thoughts and Questions

Are you encountering severe trials? Do you let the pain drive you to Him? Are you asking Him, "What are you trying to teach me through this?"

Dear sister, hold tight to His hand and let Him wipe your tears, comfort your hurting heart, and walk you through to victory! When you do, you, like Joseph, can say, "What was meant for evil, God meant for good."

Prayer

Father, when tragedy strikes, help me to remember that you are walking that road with me. Thank you for your great compassion. Thank you that you not only see my tears, but that you also hurt with me and collect my tears in a bottle. You are truly a good Father—and I am so glad that I am your child. Amen.

Dig Drainage Ditches

Be anxious for nothing,
but in everything by prayer and supplication
with thanksgiving let your requests
be made known to God.
And the peace of God,
which surpasses all comprehension,
will guard your hearts and your minds
in Christ Jesus.
—PHILIPPIANS 4:6–7

IN CONSTRUCTION, NOTHING IS WORSE THAN A JOB SITE BOGGED down in mud. You can hardly walk through it, and you surely can't drive through it. It's a nuisance, it's frustrating, and it slows the building process.

Stress and anxiety are a lot like mud—they too are frustrating, and they slow the forward progress. Stress and anxiety, however, are much more dangerous than mere job-site mud. Stress can kill.

On a job site, proper drainage is vitally important. The ground must be contoured so rainwater is diverted around or away from the building so a large amount of water doesn't accumulate where it shouldn't. And sometimes we must dig drainage ditches that pull the water away from the building project to keep it mud free.

Likewise, our spiritual remodeling job site must have proper drainage.

What are "spiritual drainage ditches"? They're ideas and practices that, when implemented, divert excess stress and worry away from us and prevent a large amount of it from accumulating where it shouldn't be. These ideas, which keep stress from stealing our attention away from God and family, could very well save both our physical and spiritual lives.

According to Philippians 4:6–7, we are to counter anxiety, stress, and worry with prayer, supplication, and thanksgiving. These are our spiritual drainage ditches.

All three of these could be described as a type of prayer. *Petition* prayers are prayers prayed on behalf of others or to address certain situations, whether those situations are related to the world (famine, leadership), family members, or health. *Supplication* payers are prayers prayed on behalf of ourselves: prayers for guidance, forgiveness, mercy, salvation, deliverance, or healing. *Thanksgiving* prayers are prayers that give God glory for all He has done in our lives. We are to remember often what He has done on our behalf, tell others about them, and always give Him complete glory.

God wants us free from stress and worry. He wants us to have peace. In fact, the opposite of stress is *peace*, and God is the author of peace. Christ is the Lord of peace and the Prince of Peace. Peace is a fruit of the Holy Spirit, and peace accompanies faith and righteousness. Shalom peace is wholeness or well-being inside our souls. Luke 12:27–28 says, "Consider the lilies, how they grow: they neither toil nor spin.... But if God so clothes the grass in the field, which is alive today and tomorrow is thrown into the furnace, how much more will He clothe you?"

Recognizing our stress overload signals is important. When my children were small and diapers, messes, and slobber got to me, I recognized my overload warnings and knew I had to deal with the stress in a constructive way. I needed a de-stresser to keep from escalating into an even more uptight situation—even if that meant going out on the deck for a few peaceful breaths of fresh air or eating a pint of ice cream. Fresh air and ice cream were the perfect de-stressers.

Final Thoughts and Questions

What are your warning signs? Do you listen to them and do something to divert the stress? One way is by doing something solely for you, something you love to do. It's okay to take care of yourself so you can take care of everyone else. Do whatever you have to do to ditch the stress. But remember to do it guilt free. Otherwise you've missed the whole point.

Prayer

Father, I trust You with my everything. I give You the burdens of others, and I give You my problems. Help me to remember all the blessings You've bestowed on me. Help me to always give You the glory for the blessings in my life, and help me tell the world of all the blessings You've poured out on me. Amen.

Day Sixty-Three

Clean Up the Site

Who may ascend into the hill of the LORD?
And who may stand in His holy place?
He who has clean hands and a pure heart,
who has not lifted up his soul to falsehood
and has not sworn deceitfully.
—PSALM 24:3–4

IT'S AMAZING HOW DIRTY A JOB SITE CAN GET. IF WE DON'T STAY on top of it, the messes can get completely out of hand. Not only do they make the site look unprofessional, but they can affect both the speed and quality of work. Too much stuff lying around makes it difficult to find the tools and materials you need to get the job done right and on time. Sometimes the messes require only a little sweeping and picking up; other times they require a pressure washer, a bottle of bleach, and a giant dumpster.

Our spiritual lives too sometimes need some cleaning up. When we've allowed our spiritual temples to become cluttered, it harms us spiritually. It allows the Enemy to kick us around. If too much garbage is lying around (lies of the Enemy, false teachings, sins we've allowed to enter our lives, addictions, self-serving justifications), we can't find the truth of God's Word to help us find victory and success.

Here's why it's so important to clean up our spiritual ground. We're made in the very image of God Himself, which means at the core of our being is God's DNA. A spark of Almighty God is living and glowing inside all of us. We are His dwelling place, His holy temple. We must honor Him by keeping our cores clean and pure.

A temple has two main purposes: a place of prayer and a place devoted to the service of God. In the Old Testament, when Moses dedicated the tabernacle to God, God's glorious presence came down and filled it with smoke. Numbers 9:15 tells us the smoke had the appearance of fire all that evening until morning. When Solomon dedicated the newly constructed temple to God, a cloud so thick it kept the priests from doing their duties filled it. When we dedicate our lives to Christ, our bodies become the temples where the Holy Spirit indwells like a thick cloud of glory.

The only thing that separates a church from any other building in the neighborhood is the presence of God. The only thing that separates our bodies from the rest of the bodies in the world is the presence of God's Spirit in our temples. Do we allow God's presence to be readily visible, or have we allowed our temples to get messy? Have we defiled our temples by serving self instead of God and others? Have we disobeyed God's commands or offered ourselves up in sin? Do we care for the things of this world more than we care for the things of God? Have we sworn deceitfully or offered up falsehoods? If so, it's time to roll up our sleeves and get busy cleaning.

Cleaning our temples means repenting of our sins, obeying God's Word by following the example set by Christ, and submitting our will to God's will. Then we ask the Holy Spirit to come and dwell inside us. Since we've invited deity into our being, then our lives must reflect His presence by living a life of purity and righteousness—a life that perfectly reflects the actions and words of Christ.

Final Thoughts and Questions

How does it make you feel knowing that God's DNA is at the core of your being? Will this affect your behavior toward others? How clean is your spiritual job site? What lies have you let in? Name them and repent of them. Allow the Holy Spirit to wash you clean.

Prayer

Father, show me areas in my spiritual life I have allowed to become polluted. I repent of them, and I ask You to wash me clean and help me be more like Jesus in these areas. Amen.

Completion and Final Inspection

The day Christ calls us home to heaven and we stand before Him to give account of every thought, every word, and every action is when our spiritual construction days are complete. When we've remodeled our spiritual lives to look exactly like Christ, we can be confident that we've done a good job and will have nothing to worry about when we're called to account. Our sins are covered by the shed blood of our Savior, Jesus Christ, and our transformation process is complete.

This is when we wait with longing to hear the Father say, "Well done, good and faithful servant!... Come and share your master's happiness." (Matt. 25:21 NIV*)*

What Should My Finished Project Look Like?

You also, as living stones, are being built up as
a spiritual house for a holy priesthood,
to offer up spiritual sacrifices acceptable
to God through Jesus Christ.
—1 PETER 2:5

WHAT DO YOU WANT YOUR FINISHED SPIRITUAL HOUSE TO LOOK like? A beautiful temple or a makeshift tent? Tents are okay for camping, but they get tiresome *very* quickly. Sleeping on the ground with mosquitoes buzzing all night and hearing loud birds singing at the top of their lungs at four thirty in the morning makes me quickly yearn for my memory foam mattress in my nice cozy home!

I don't know about you, but I'm pushing on toward perfection because I don't want to spend eternity in a tent. I want my spiritual remodel to be something breathtaking, sturdy, and functional. Maybe even with an ocean view. I want it to be perfection itself.

Christ instructed us, "Be perfect, therefore, as your heavenly Father is perfect" (Matt. 5:48 NIV). YAHWEH is the standard of perfection, and Christ shows us how to live out that perfection. But what is perfection really? Is it living a flawless life? Living 100 percent in service to God? Not sinning?

I believe spiritual perfection looks like this: selflessly loving each other, especially the unlovable, our enemies, those who hate us, and even those who mistreat us, even when our lives are a mess and a work in progress.

The Bible is full of examples of how God used ordinary work-in-progress people to love on the unlovable as a means of changing the world. The twelve disciples were a bunch of everyday dudes, and King David was an ordinary shepherd. Yet God used all these ordinary guys in extraordinary ways. The disciples brought the message of salvation through faith in the Messiah, Jesus Christ, to the whole world. King David, the most famous king in history, wrote beautiful poetry that points us to the Messiah.

These everyday people all had a few things in common. They were all selflessly obedient to God's will, they all had a personal relationship with Him, and they were committed to God even though obstacles were in their path (such as persecution, loss, and, in David's case, an angry king chasing him all over the countryside). Their lives were not picture-perfect; one could even call many of them dysfunctional. Yet these folks were all courageous people willing to take great risks for God even while they were still working to transform their lives according to His will.

Together with God, they built their spiritual temples into structures that were stunning creations of beauty. Together with God, they selflessly loved and served others. Together with God, their finished projects were ornate and lavish temples as close to perfection as they could possibly make them.

Prayer

Father God, I am a willing vessel, however far from perfect my life is. But regardless of my imperfections, please use me for Your service. Lead me to the ones who need salvation, lead me to the ones who are hurting and needy, and lead me to the ones who are broken and searching for You. Give me wisdom to say the right words to lead them into Your kingdom. Amen.

Day Sixty-Five

Room-by-Room Inspection

Examine me, O LORD, and try me;
test my mind and my heart.
—PSALM 26:2

WHEN A BUILDING INSPECTOR COMES TO A CONSTRUCTION JOB SITE, he examines many things. On the outside, he looks at the foundation, the drainage, and the overall structure. On the inside, he looks at plumbing, electricity, and wall placement. He also does a room-by-room inspection to make sure everything was built to code.

Spiritually speaking, God is the building inspector who performs a room-by-room inspection of our hearts. It's up to Him whether we pass or fail.

We each come programmed with various rooms in our hearts. We all have a motive room, a faith room, an attitude room, an affections room, a conscience room, a memory room, and a planning room. These are the rooms we want to have in extra good shape for God's inspection. In Psalm 26:2, David prayed this amazing prayer: "Examine me, O LORD, and try me; test my mind and my heart."

I used to sing and play guitar on the worship team at my church. When I started on the team, I really loved it, and I had a sincere desire to use my gifts to worship God. I can't tell you exactly when that motive to worship God morphed into an "I hope everyone is impressed with me" motive. It was a sly and sneaky move I did not see coming. Slowly I moved from praising God to hoping others were noticing me, which, looking back, scares me. It's the very sin Satan was guilty of.

I got busy and dealt with that motive. I acknowledged it was there, I laid it before Christ, and I repented with all my heart. I let God, the building inspector, perform a room inspection on my heart.

The *motive* room is where the heart gets its inspiration and desire to be like Christ. We need to let God get in there and take a look around. He sees through all the playacting and the smiles clear through to the motive. It isn't enough to *do* good. He wants good deeds, yes, but with good thoughts that stem from good motives. With God, it all starts with the heart.

The *faith* room is where we find the strength to take action to be Christlike. Let's allow the Holy Spirit to point out our faith's strengths and weaknesses.

In the *attitude* room, Christ invites us to deny our natural responses and replace them with Christlike, selfless responses, such as

- being poor in spirit,
- mourning over sin,
- being meek,
- hungering after righteousness,
- showing mercy,
- being pure in heart,
- being a peacemaker, and
- being willing to be persecuted for the sake of righteousness.

These are the attitudes that please the Father. They remind us that this earthly kingdom is fleeting, but God's kingdom is eternal, and therefore we should focus on the eternal.

When we let God inspect every aspect of our hearts, we allow Him to work perfection in us. So anticipate the day when He will sign off on your inspection report, stating to the world and to the myriads upon myriads of heavenly bodies that you have passed His inspection.

Can you even imagine the exhilaration of that day? That day is coming!

Prayer

Father, inspect my heart. Shine a spotlight on my sins, bad motives, weak faith, and wicked attitudes. Make me clean. Make me pure and spotless. I love You and want to please You in all my ways. Amen.

Day Sixty-Six

Am I Done Yet?

Let us not lose heart in doing good,
for in due time we will reap if we do not grow weary.
—GALATIANS 6:9

MY LIFE USED TO BE ONE LONG MARATHON FROM SUNUP TO SUN-down. With five children, there were endless dirty dishes, laundry, and homework assignments needing my undivided attention. Now my nest is nearly empty, and the race has wound down. In fact, time seems to drag. I rarely cook, there isn't much to clean, and there's not much laundry to do. I admit that sometimes I feel unneeded.

But I know God has more for me. As one season comes to a close, another is beginning. As I write this book and run our ministry, I don't yet know exactly what all this new season requires of me, but I do know prayer is a big part of it. I carry some heavy burdens I can do nothing about except pray, so pray I will! I'm also dusting off and reanalyzing dreams I set aside years ago, and I'm looking forward to my future because I know God is not done with me.

God is not through with you either. He has more work for you to do. You are an important factor in His overall world-saving plan.

For most of us, this knowledge is comforting. But for some of you, the awareness that God wants more from you is unwelcome. You're weary of toiling, of effort, of trials. You just want to be done with the hardships.

If you want to give up, I challenge you to ask yourself some tough questions: *What dreams have I put on the back burner that can now be dreamed again? What is Father speaking to my heart? What burdens do I carry that can be given to Father God in a stronger, more prayerful way? What needs do I see in my family, my neighborhood, my church, and my nation that I can do something about?*

When we fight the temptation to throw in the towel and keep pressing on with whatever the Father places on our hearts, we're ready to head out with our work boots on. The joy of being used by Father God to build His kingdom here on earth; the joy of leading lost souls back to their source, YAHWEH; the joy of working alongside the Holy Spirit to accomplish the Father's perfect will; the joy of living a righteous life (meaning one that resembles Christ); and the greatest reward of all—a face-to-face relationship with Christ and an eternity of basking in the presence of our good Father—are all great rewards for not giving up!

Final Thoughts and Questions

Keep dreaming of your future. Even if life is bleak right now, trust that it will be better soon. Keep on planning, dreaming, analyzing, and scheming. Don't stop. Don't even slow down, because there is much work to do before our King returns.

Prayer

Father, bring to my mind dreams and ambitions I long ago set on the shelf. Give me a vision again. Give me a passion to do Your work. I will be Your hands and Your feet, so take me where You will. Amen.

Day Sixty-Seven

Now I See Dimly

We know in part and we prophesy in part; but when the perfect
comes, the partial will be done away. When I was a child,
I used to speak like a child, think like a child, reason like a child;
when I became a man, I did away with childish things.
For now we see in a mirror dimly, but then face to face;
now I know in part, but then I will know fully
just as I also have been fully known.
—1 CORINTHIANS 13:9–12

THE REALM WHERE YAHWEH OUR FATHER LIVES AND OPERATES
is beyond our comprehension. Here is a quick glimpse:

> Behold, the LORD God will come with might, with His arm
> [Christ] ruling for Him.... Like a shepherd He will tend his
> flock, in His arm He will gather the lambs and carry them in his
> bosom; He will gently lead the nursing ewes. Who has measured
> the waters in the hollow of his hand. (Isa. 40:10–12)

God's hand can hold all the waters of the universe! It is also written
that all the dirt of earth can fit into His measuring cup (Isa. 40:12).
Furthermore, He has scales that weigh all the hills and all the mountains. That is *big*. In what He has done and is continuing to do, God
is gigantic. He has absolute power, wisdom, and intelligence. Nobody
taught Him how. Nobody created Him, because He is the creator!

"He counts the number of the stars; He gives names to all of them.
Great is our Lord and abundant in strength; His understanding is
infinite" (Ps. 147:4–5). Do you have any idea how many stars are in

214

the universe? More than 10 to the 24th power (that's a 1 with 24 zeros after it). Scientists get that number from theorizing that more than 170 billion galaxies stretch out 13.8 billion light years from earth in every direction and multiplying that number by the number of stars in our own galaxy. So pardon my math, because it is and always has been horrible, but if 50 billion people make it to God's kingdom and He splits the stars up evenly among us, we would each get 200 billion stars to explore and rule (according to www.esa.int). Wow!

As if that isn't enough, He has storehouses filled with snow and hail—just in case of a snow and hail shortage. He knows the number of hairs on each person's head; He even knows if a sparrow falls. God is un-comprehendible. We can grasp Him only dimly because our brains would short out if we saw His magnitude. And remember, He isn't done creating yet. The universe keeps growing. He is still at work upholding all things by His power.

We are *so very lowly* compared to Him. Yet in all of our lowliness, He still loves us. That fact alone makes God magnificent.

Yes, now I see dimly, but one day I will see Him face-to-face—without melting.

Prayer

Father, thank You for loving me. You are so amazing. I worship You! Open my eyes to see more of Your greatness today. Amen.

Day Sixty-Eight

Crown of Life

Blessed is a man who perseveres under trial;
for once he has been approved,
he will receive the crown of life
which the Lord has promised those who love Him.
—JAMES 1:12

DID YOU KNOW CROWNS CARRY A LOT OF MEANING? THEY'RE A SYMbol of authority, political legitimacy, prestige, ownership, victory, and nobility. Crowns are a sign of extremely high value.

The New Testament mentions three different crowns disciples of Jesus Christ will have the privilege to wear: the crown of righteousness, the crown of glory, and the crown of life. Each crown is an eternal reward we receive for serving God. Each crown is a token of everlasting love, something like a wedding ring.

When we allow the trials of this hard life to perfect our faith, and we submit ourselves to God's will and work hard to transform our image into the image of the Master, Jesus Christ, God in His rich and abundant mercy places upon our heads the crown of life. Revelation 2 tells us those who do God's will to the end are going to wear the crown of life.

Are we willing to face ridicule or public shame? Matthew 16:25 says, "Whoever wishes to save his life will lose it; but whoever loses his life for My sake will find it."

Are we willing to face family conflict, give up earthly advantages, and lose ourselves for the sake of following Christ? Matthew 10:36–37 says, "A man's enemies will be the members of his household. He who loves father or mother more than Me is not worthy of Me; and he who loves son or daughter more than Me is not worthy of Me."

Being Christ's disciple requires a full-time life of sacrifice. When life gets hard, when we have trials, when life disappoints us, when family members cut us off because we have chosen God's kingdom, when we lose our jobs because of our no-compromise God-fearing beliefs, when we face death because of our love and service to Almighty God, we must remember this: those who love the Father and fearlessly serve Him will be rewarded with the victorious crown of life.

Jesus wore the cross so we could wear the crown.

Final Thoughts and Questions

Joshua trees grow only in harsh desert conditions. They grow slowly and are unusually bent and gnarled, but they flourish in the desert's ruthless conditions because their root systems stretch deep beneath the rocks to find any pockets of moisture far below.

When you persevere through the trials of life, you are like these hardy little trees. You send your roots down deep to the source of life and can thrive in whatever conditions God places you in. You may be bent and gnarled by the world's harsh environment, yet you will stubbornly grow toward heaven.

Prayer

Blessed Eternal One, I send my roots down deep into Your love, truth, peace, and faithfulness. You are my source of life. Help me always to look to You as I go through this challenging life. Amen.

Occupancy Certificate

"Do not let your heart be troubled; believe in God,
believe also in Me. In my Father's house are many dwelling places;
if it were not so, I would have told you; for I go to prepare
a place for you. If I go and prepare a place for you,
I will come again and receive you to Myself, that where I am,
there you may be also."
—JOHN 14:1–3

THERE ONCE WAS A WEALTHY CHRISTIAN WOMAN WHO GAVE TO the needy. But when she gave, it was with a stingy, tight fist. In contrast, her poor, hardworking cook gave to the needy with a generous, open hand. Both these women died and went to heaven. As an angel escorted the wealthy woman to her heavenly home, they passed a beautiful mansion.

"Whose home is this?" she asked her escort.

"This is your cook's home," the angel replied.

If my servant has such a fantastic home, the woman silently reasoned, *my home will be ten times as fabulous.*

Imagine her horror when the angel led her to a cardboard box. "This is outrageous!" the woman spewed.

"I'm sorry, ma'am," the angel gently replied. "We did the best we could with the materials you sent us."

Our earthly actions determine our heavenly status. Are we sending an abundant quantity of excellent building components to heaven so

God can build us beautiful mansions? Or are we sending just enough to make cardboard boxes?

God's kingdom is real! The whole Bible is a story about His kingdom. God has promised it. It's where we'll get our new, pain-free, wrinkle-free, fat-free eternal bodies to wrap around our eternal souls. In God's kingdom we will walk on streets of transparent gold, catch the waves on the crystal sea, eat amazing fruit from amazing trees (whose leaves produce oil that will heal the nations), walk through gates of solid pearl, worship God face-to-face, fly, take eternity to explore the universe, party with friends and family for days on end, do cartwheels, write music, paint masterpieces, run real fast, love completely, enjoy everything, be like Christ, have profound peace, and do everything we could ever imagine and more! God's kingdom is His dwelling place, the home to His angels and His Son, Jesus. Kingdom living is going to be *perfect*!

But our status in heaven depends heavily on our actions here on earth. What have we been doing and what do we need to continue to do to send quality building materials to God?

The answer is simple. It is what this entire book has been about: be like Jesus in every tiny area of your life. Love as He loved. Think as He thought. Speak as He spoke. Serve as He served. Forgive as He forgave. Obey as He obeyed. Help the hurting, give to the poor, visit prisoners, bind the wounds of the brokenhearted, save lives, be a light, push back the darkness, and live as if you are already in God's kingdom.

Final Thoughts and Questions

Imagine what your heavenly mansion will look like. Do you think you're sending enough proper materials to build it? How can you begin today to increase the output and quality of your spiritual materials?

Prayer

Oh, King of the Universe, help me to send up to you valuable building materials so that you can build for me my heavenly dream home. I long for your Kingdom. But give me eyes to see the needs of those around me and ears to hear your leading as I continue to live here on earth. Amen.

Day Seventy

Keeping Your Eyes
on the Skies

*"Let us rejoice and be glad and give the glory to Him,
for the marriage of the Lamb has come and His bride
has made herself ready." It was given to her to clothe herself
in fine linen, bright and clean; for the fine linen
is the righteous acts of the saints.*
—REVELATION 19:7–8

THE RETURN OF JESUS WILL SURELY HAPPEN. HE PROMISED IT! THE early church longed for it, and we eagerly anticipate it today. Even though Christ has tarried, we can have confident faith that He will return. When the Bible talks about the return of Christ, it refers to us as His bride. I always thought that curious until I researched ancient Hebrew wedding traditions.

First a bride was chosen by the groom's father. (Jesus said, "You did not choose Me but I chose you" [John 15:16]). Then the groom's father sent his son to the bride's home with three important things: the bride price, the Ketubah, and a new skin of wine.

The bride price was usually a large amount of money, proportionate to the love and value the groom felt for his bride. ("You were bought with a price" [1 Cor. 6:20 RSV]. The price we were bought with was Jesus's precious blood.)

Then the groom presented the bride's father with the Ketubah, a document that stated all the promises he was making to his bride. This Ketubah was the contract of the marriage covenant. (Spiritually, our Ketubah is all the teachings of the Messiah—Jesus Christ.) If the bride consented to these terms, all parties of the contract drank of the new wine to seal the marriage covenant. At this point they were betrothed to each other and considered husband and wife.

Next, the groom went away to make a dwelling place for his beloved. (Jesus said, "I go and prepare a place for you" [John 14:3]). He worked diligently to build a nice home for his bride so when it was completed he could return to take her home with him. While waiting, the bride learned everything she could about her beloved. She learned how to please him and how to be the perfect wife. And even if his returning was delayed, she remained faithful. Finally, the joyful day arrived. (Jesus said, "You also must be ready, because the Son of Man will come at an hour when you do not expect him" [Matt. 24:44 NIV].)

The second part of the ceremony was the home-taking. The groom took his bride to his home over which he had tirelessly labored. Together they joined the guests for the wedding feast.

> "Hallelujah!
> For our Lord God Almighty reigns.
> Let us rejoice and be glad
> and give him glory!
> For the wedding of the Lamb has come,
> and his bride has made herself ready.
> Fine linen, bright and clean,
> was given her to wear."

(Fine linen stands for the righteous acts of God's holy people.)

Then the angel said to me, "Write this: Blessed are those who are invited to the wedding supper of the Lamb!" (Rev. 19:6–9 NIV)

I love this illustration. It's everything we long for as believers. It's our future! It's our hope! It's also a perfect picture of what we need to be doing while we're waiting for His return—making ourselves ready for Him.

As we daily remodel our spiritual homes, we must keep our eyes on the sky with great expectation for the return of the Bridegroom! We must take this time to learn all we can about Him and learn to be the perfect "wife." And as we wait, we must build beautiful spiritual lives that are pure and spotless. Even if He tarries, we must faithfully wait, because blessed are those who are called to the marriage supper of the Lamb. And blessed are those who are ready and waiting for Him.

Hallelujah—come, Lord Jesus!

Final Thoughts and Questions

Your robe is spotless and without wrinkle when you're a perfect mirror reflection of Jesus. The time of His return is near. All the signs He told us to look for are coming true, so your time on this earth may not be long. Are you using that time wisely? Are you looking more and more like Jesus every day? Are you telling others? Are you sharing the good news?

Prayer

Oh, blessed Father, help me to be faithful to my spiritual groom— Jesus Christ—as I wait for Him. Help me to learn everything I can about Him, and help me as I work hard to become transformed into his image. Jesus—Yeshua, my redeemer—I love you. May you find me adorned in a white gleaming robe when you return for me. Come quickly, my husband and King—I long for you! Amen.

Dear sister, I have so enjoyed spending this time with you. I love you! I thank you for hearing my thoughts and encouragements as we spiritually build together. Keep up the good work. Time is short. Keep your eyes on the skies—our King is coming! The marriage supper of the Lamb is nigh!

Prayer Journal

Prayer Journal

Prayer Journal

Prayer Journal

Prayer Journal